THE TAVERN
OF **POPRICANI**

THE TAVERN OF POPRICANI

Yitskhok Horowitz

TRANSLATED FROM THE YIDDISH BY
Ollie Elkus

ILLUSTRATIONS BY
Ezra Finkin

Naydus Press
Cincinnati, Ohio
2022

Published 2022 by Naydus Press
Printed in the United States of America
Cover design by Lindsay Lake
Cover illustration courtesy of the Jewish Museum of Greece. (Haim Nahmias' tavern in Ioannina, around 1930. The owner is having a drink with his friend Panayiotis Panagopoulos, a member of the town's military band. ©Photographic archive of the Jewish Museum of Greece.)

First Edition

Naydus Press is a non-profit, 501(c)(3) organization dedicated to increasing awareness of and access to Yiddish literature by supporting Yiddish translators and publishing their translations into English. Our goal is to bring the best of Yiddish literature to new generations of readers.

A Yiddish Book Center Translation

ISBN 978-1-7341936-1-9

This book is dedicated to my father,

whose life lessons will, as Yitskhok put it,

"forever accompany me as a light upon my path."

CONTENTS

ACKNOWLEDGEMENTS

Throughout the process of translating a book and bringing it to press there are many moments. The first moment is when you stumble upon the book, like meeting a friend for the first time, completely unaware how intertwined your lives are about to become. This is quite a special moment, although you don't realize it. Then you realize it, and that's the next moment, when you start to entertain the idea of translating the book, and you feel something. It's a feeling that descends upon you, and whose cosmic nature even the most cynical of translators would be reluctant to deny. There are the micro-moments too; the moments of doubt, and hesitation, and questioning that follow these moments of endeavor, but these micro-moments are there as if only to emphasize the elation of the larger, more grand and momentous moments of achievement yet to come.

The first of the momentous moments, in my case, was the moment when the Yiddish Book Center accepted me and this project for a translation fellowship. Had that not happened, it's more than likely this book never would have been published. I have many people to thank for this, starting with Mindl Cohen, Margaret Frothingham, Abigail Weaver, and everyone else at the Yiddish Book Center. I have had nothing but wonderful experiences with them, and the fellowship has been the foundation for so much amazing Yiddish literature in translation, and a structure of support not only for me but for so many other Yiddish translators, including my mentor Daniel Kennedy. Daniel, by the way, is the next person to thank, and a very important one at that.

Having never had a mentor before, I didn't expect much. Daniel has certainly shaken that expectation, as he has done more than even the most entitled person would expect a mentor to do. I feel lucky to know him let alone work with him, and he has shown a belief in me and my abilities as a translator that I didn't have in myself. He is a brilliant mind and a kind soul, and his input over the course of this project has fundamentally shaped my view of translation and what it means to be a translator. There's no doubt that I will be carrying his wisdom into all of my future projects.

I've been lucky enough to have also had the eyes of many other great translators review a chapter or two of this book and lend their perspective. Some of the workshop leaders during the fellowship who offered their advice and expertise to me, and to whom I offer my humble thanks, were Sebastian Schulman, Jennifer Croft, and Katherine Silver. Katherine in particular taught me a great lesson in navigating tenses between languages in her review of the chapter, "Shabbes," going back and forth with me about it long after the workshop had ended. So a great, Shabbes-sized thanks to Katherine.

Then there are my fellow fellows, Annie Kaufman, Moyshe Zeilengold, Jonah and Jonathan Boyarin, Leyzer Burko, Sonia Gollance, Matthew Johnson, Shahar Fineberg, Miriam Isaacs, and Beth Dwoskin, all of whom have contributed their thoughts and creative efforts to this book, and I must thank them all for that and the many words of encouragement shared with me along the way. The whole experiential aspect of a workshop is certainly sculpted by the people you are working with, and I couldn't have asked for a better, more supportive group of individuals.

Then there was life after the fellowship, when the nice folks who raised me at the Yiddish Book Center sent me out into the world to find a publisher. This was the next momentous moment, when Naydus Press agreed to publish the book, and Jordan Finkin became my editor. After having spent a whole year workshopping the book during the fellowship, changing things once, twice, and three times, only to change them back again, it was certainly difficult to see Jordan cut it to pieces. As Jordan knows full well, after spending this much time on a book, certain words, concepts, and turns of phrase which have been there since the beginning start to crystallize. We become stubborn, they become immalleable in our minds, and it grows difficult to tell whether it's because they are the way they should be, or simply because we come to expect them to be the way they've always been. Nevertheless, as someone who takes translation extremely personally, it was a great lesson in compromise working with Jordan, and he was always sensitive to my attachment to the book. Through drafts on drafts, edits over edits, and cyclical conversations, his patient and diligent work made *The Tavern of Popricani* an infinitely better book. I must give my heartfelt thanks to Jordan Finkin for believing in it, and in me, and for being open to the compromise between us that has made *The Tavern of Popricani* the wonderful book I believe it to be.

As I finish writing these words of thanks, which have truly been a perfect opportunity for reflecting on each little moment I've shared with this book, I also think ahead, to the final momentous moment: the moment it's published, and in my hand, and I'm most likely noticing, and obsessing about that one tiny thing I wish I had changed before it went to press. This will no doubt be a sweet moment, and it has me thinking about you, the reader. There are so many books out there that you could be reading, and that is precisely the issue when deciding to translate something. We are overwhelmed with content, we can't translate it all, and you can't read it all. But like I said, I felt something when I read this book, and so I followed that. I believed in it, the nice folks at the Yiddish Book Center believed in it, Jordan believed in it, and I hope you sense that belief while reading it. Either way, I'd like to offer my advance thanks to you, the reader, for making time to read, among all other books, this very book, at this very moment. A most sincere thank you.

Naydus Press wishes to express its gratitude to its editorial board; to the Jewish Museum of Greece and its Director, Zanet Battinou; and to the following for their financial support:

Delphine Katz
The Yiddish Book Center

INTRODUCTION

The biography of Yitskhok (Isac) Horowitz (1893–1961) makes for familiar reading, proceeding as it does along lines similar to many American Yiddish writers of the early 20th century: small-town upbringing in Eastern Europe; immigration to the United States; manual or menial labor while engaging in intellectual pursuits and honing their craft, often for the Yiddish press; and the eventual blossoming of a mature talent. It is a formula that worked for so many, as it did for Horowitz.

Born in Epureni in eastern Romania, Horowitz was educated in Iași, Romania's cultural capital and the heartland of professional Yiddish theater. In the absence of detailed historical material it is tempting to see a young Horowitz bitten by the Yiddish cultural bug during his time in the city. What we do know is that eventually, at the age of fifteen, he went to help his father at his tavern in the village of Popricani, north of Iași. From there, in 1909, Horowitz came to New York where for three years he worked in the city's sweatshops. There he began his literary endeavors, publishing poetry in Yiddish newspapers.

It was in the Yiddish press that he found his escape from the sweatshops, as both author and editor. But it was also in the press that he found his activist voice for vegetarian causes. He variously edited or contributed to Yiddish vegetarian publications, including *Der vegetaryer* (The Vegetarian), *Di vegetarisher velt* (Vegetarian World), and *Der naturist un vegetaryer* (The Naturalist and Vegetarian). Not only that, but during the First World War he lobbied the United States government to excuse vegetarians from military service, arguing that their beliefs precluded them from combat. His convictions also found an outlet in creative work, notably with the vegetarian-themed play *Dos kol fun di shtume* (The Voice of the Mute, 1920).

Horowitz produced a varied body of work. In addition to his work as an editor, he penned a number of plays for both adult as well as juvenile audiences; works of criticism, including about the Yiddish writer Moyshe Nadir (1885–1943) and the Romanian writer Panait Istrati (1884–1935); translations into Yiddish from several languages, many from Romanian (including works of Ronetti Roman [1847–1908], Vasile Morțun [1860–1919], and Vasile Pop [1875–1931]), but also perhaps most famously Kahlil Gibran's *The Prophet*. (A letter from Gibran to Horowitz attests to how warmly the translation was received.) And of course there is this book—*The Tavern of Popricani*—the memoir of his childhood, first published in 1953.

Perhaps it was due in part to his experience writing for children, but the voice Horowitz develops for his child-self in *The Tavern of Popricani* is both believable and affectively effective. In the literary voice of young Horowitz, a child of undefined age, we encounter a kind of faux naïf. The author Horowitz writes as an adult but *through* a child's eyes, trying to conjure up the vivid portrait of a life and landscape half a world away and at forty-five years' remove.

While neither a Bildungsroman nor an adventure tale, the book does describe the kinds of moments likely to imprint themselves on a child's memory: the first longed-for and worked-for object (in this case a fiddle); the terror of the deep and the dark (here the tavern's wine cellar); the death of a beloved animal (as in the old mare); humiliation at being laughed at by one's family (when he steals what he mistakenly believes to be cookies); and so forth. There are moments of adventure as well, as in the chapter "Wolves." The tale of Kiva the baker, for instance, presents the intriguing intersection of memory and literary conceit. Kiva describes a trip he took to deliver bread and bagels to the tavern. Pursued through the wilderness by wolves, it was only by tossing out piecemeal his load of loaves and bagels that he could delay the wolves long enough to make it to the village and to safety. I am put in mind of a story ("Another Bride") by the Yiddish writer Fradl Shtok in which one of the characters recounts his experience being chased on his sled by a pack of wolves, and it was only by casting off, one by one, his load of geese that he staved off his impending doom. I do not know what the Urtext of this story might be (or whether Horowitz was a youthful devotee of Jack London), but it seems a literary topos, and both a dramatic and entertaining one at that.

Whether we consider Horowitz's book literature-qua-memoir or memoir-qua-literature, it participates in a literary tradition that spans modern Yiddish literature's history from Mendele Moykher Sforim (1835–1917) to Isaac Bashevis Singer (1904–1991). While *The Tavern of Popricani* does not share Bashevis's exoticism or eroticism, nor Mendele's lyricism, it does offer an intimacy and sincerity that make for enjoyable, and often indeed charming, reading.

One of the values of this book is the light it shines on a region of the Eastern European Jewish landscape that is not well represented in English translation, namely the villages of Romania. The Popricani of Horowitz's childhood was not a shtetl, the Yiddish demographic heartland. Rather, it was a village tucked away in the countryside (and, from the narrator's perspective, wilderness) of Romania. What's more, the tavern at the center of the story was not even in the village itself but on its outskirts. This was a place where the narrator and his family were the only Jews in sight. And through his child's eyes it is an existence both secure and, ironically, precarious. The dramatic final chapter, "The Bull," with its palpable menace of anti-Semitism during the Peasants' Revolt of 1907, unsettlingly punctures the idyll of his childhood.

But it is the Jewishness in the story that makes for the most beguiling reading. Their household is a Jewish world in which religion is a form, not a substance. It is something quaint, to be humored but not taken too seriously. The Sabbath, observed as a matter of course, is treated as something far more familial than theological, more cultural than cultic. Even Hebrew in a religious context is an alien tongue. In Horowitz's words, for example, on the Sabbath "our mother always wanted to hear some hymns, or what she called *'zmires'* [. . .] We children didn't know what *'zmires'* meant." For all that, however, the family's Yiddishkeit remains an unquestionable feature of its identity. (And it is only in a world seen through Jewish eyes that wolves can be placated with bagels.) Ultimately, for a man with a peripatetic biography like Horowitz, his memoir is both a story, and a literary enactment, of rootedness. And it's a story whose emotional authenticity grows richly from those roots.

—*The Editor*

TRANSLATOR'S FOREWORD

It's common to assume translations are about words. The thinking might be that when you pick the right word, you'll have the right translation. However, translations are more about images and feelings than words. The words may be the instrument, but the images and feelings are the substance. When the image and feeling evoked by the translation are those of the original, that's when you know the words are right. This may be an over-simplification, but nevertheless a useful guiding principle to keep in mind while translating.

My hope is that, through the images and feelings evoked by this translation of *The Tavern of Popricani*, we have created a world as immersive in the English as it is in the Yiddish. If we haven't done that, I'd like to believe we have at least created a piece of literature that can be read as an "original" in its own right, standing firm alongside the Yiddish text that inspired it. To that end, if you wish to simply start from the first chapter and disregard this foreword, you would be very welcome. But for those with an interest in translation, I will detail some of the idiosyncrasies of translating this particular book, as well as some of the "untranslatables" found along the way.

As it happens, Yitskhok Horowitz was quite an accomplished literary translator himself, which comes as no surprise, given that his childhood was spent negotiating constant shifts between Yiddish and Romanian. This skill was put to good use in *The Tavern of Popricani*, as the book was already part-translation. That is to say, although it was written completely in Yiddish (save for a few Romanian flavor words), many of the characters are gentile Romanians, so a great deal of the dialogue in the book is a Romanian-to-Yiddish translation on Horowitz's part, making it a sort of translated translation on mine.

An amusing example of this is his rendering of the phrase "*vi ikh bin a krist,*" a modification of the common Yiddish idiom "*vi ikh bin a yid,*" which means literally "as I am a Jew" and figuratively something along the lines of "as sure as I'm standing here before you." Adapting the phrase for Mihalache, a gentile Romanian peasant and protagonist of chapter nine, "The Snake," Horowitz simply swaps "*yid*" (Jew) for "*krist*" (Christian), cheekily tweaking the idiom with a humor plain to a Yiddish reader but not easily captured in English translation without an explanation as verbose as this one. Prioritizing voice over all else, you'll find the phrase rendered as "swear to Christ," as it is most idiomatic for the English and also evokes the religious imagery of the original.

While workshopping some of these passages during a Yiddish Book Center translation fellowship, much discussion was had about the handling of the words "*shikselekh*" and "*shkotsim.*" *Shikselekh* is the plural diminutive of the commonly heard "shiksa" of Jewish English, which many Americans will already be familiar with. It's essentially a not-so-affectionate way to refer to a non-Jewish woman, and "*sheygets*" (plural: *shkotsim*) is simply the lesser-known male equivalent. Both terms stem from the Hebrew root "*shekets,*" a thing of detest, a scoundrel, a rascal, a varmint. The association is no doubt harsh, but over time words wander and find new meanings. These two particular words could be used playfully, or with utter contempt, the precise level of detest to be gleaned only from context.

Within the context of *The Tavern of Popricani*, the term is used casually by the Horowitzes to refer to the gentile children of the village, and their usage seems matter of fact, more on the playful side, but with derision sometimes boiling beneath the surface. How does one capture all this in a single word? For a time I experimented with the word "scoundrels," with a gloss introducing it as a sort of pet name the Horowitzes had for the gentile children, in order to fabricate that link in the English reader's mind between scoundrels and gentiles the way it exists for the Yiddish reader. But this manner of translation would portray the usage as idiosyncratic to the Horowitz family, rather than inherent to the language. In the end, a case-by-case assessment had to be made for each usage in the text and some form of "young gentiles," "little gentiles," "gentile boys," or "gentile girls" was chosen to account for the age and gender of the gentiles in question. Although this treatment perhaps softens the sentiment and comes off less derisive than the original, it captures the otherness implied by the term, and the segregation between gentiles and Jews, which is the more essential point.

One of the finishing touches on this translation was the handling of Yitskhok's mother's favorite epithet for her children. Throughout chapter ten, "Shabbes," she bemoans her *vilde heysherikn*" (wild locusts), alluding to the plague of locusts in the book of Exodus. The cultural reference of the biblical plagues may not be lost on the English speaking world, but calling your children "wild locusts" isn't exactly idiomatic either. Simply swapping one bug for another and using "little weevils" was considered, but "vermin" seemed a better option; "weevils" was thought to sound too affectionate while "vermin" better suited the playful disdain with which his mother was speaking, and conjures up the image of the European plagues, mirroring the image of the biblical ones evoked by the original Yiddish.

Apart from these "untranslatables," and the sort of mental anguish involved in any translation, the language of *The Tavern of Popricani* may be colorful but it's actually quite simple. This was both a blessing and a curse while translating, as it wasn't ever hard to glean Horowitz's meaning, but it could be a challenge to express it properly in English. A one-for-one substitution of dictionary definitions would hardly give you the meaning intended, neglecting as it does the world of connotation and nuance that orbits Horowitz's simple language. Such a mechanical translation would be hollow and lusterless. So to capture the density of the language in *The Tavern of Popricani* it was sometimes necessary to dig deeper into the English lexicon, and, for example, employ alliteration to help capture the natural percussiveness of Yitskhok's Yiddish without departing from the simplicity of his writing. Ultimately, the book should be read fluidly and without struggle, as the original Yiddish is in no way meant to stifle the reader. A vital aspect of this book is its ability to evoke the mystic and folkloric in its imagery while its words remain straightforward and down-to-earth, and this is what I hope to have captured in the English most of all.

I.

THE TAVERN

From the outside, my father's tavern looked like a fortress. It was a large squat structure with small grated windows peering through its thick stone walls. Atop it sat an old brown shingled roof covered in moss which started at a peak and sloped low, gnarling over the musty gray walls. From the roof protruded a small round window with a dust-covered pane. At a distance it looked like the gouged gray eye of a motionless monster.

The corridor that divided the building in half was immense. Because of how large it was, the villagers told many tall tales about it. One such tale involved a villager who once rode in on an oxcart, turned the cart around in the middle of the corridor, and left without so much as a scratch on the wall. The two doors on both sides of the corridor hung on large hinges and screeched like gates. At night they were locked with heavy iron bolts and barred with long wooden poles.

The building had four rooms. Three were residential, and the fourth, on the left by the entrance, was the tavern. Truth be told, however, all the rooms served the interest of the tavern, because when it was open the boyars and the other nobles who stopped in wouldn't want to sit together with the villagers, and they'd take the other rooms.

The tavern was far from the village. Around it sprawled the boyar's expansive pastures and across from it stretched a densely wooded forest. But summer—when the peasants worked the fields, when the forest gazed over at us with its verdant overgrowth, and when all sorts of birds and other creatures whirred and warbled around the tavern—summer was so cheerful that we no longer felt how remote the tavern was.

Apart from that, summer inside the tavern was just as cheerful. Every day, villagers would arrive in ox-driven wagons, village merchants in beautifully colored carts, and boyars with lacquered droshkies and caparisoned horses. The peasants would sit at the long oak tables, treating themselves to brandy, spinning yarns and tall tales of the road, while the boyars and merchants would converse at the small tables scattered about, enjoying my mother's cooked and fried fish, and drowning themselves in wine and black Turkish coffee. And even though the boyars sat far from the merchants, and the merchants didn't mingle with the peasants, they all were still together in the same lively tavern, in the same world of summer that they all brought with them from far-off cities and villages.

But better still was Sunday. Sunday there would be no travelers, so the village peasants would no longer need to feel embarrassed and restrain their want for revelry. What's more, my father would hire two musicians on Sunday, a fiddler and a *cobzar*, to play all day long and pluck the worries and cares from the peasant's hearts.

We little children woke up much earlier than usual on Sunday. We swept and cleaned the tavern with enthusiasm, and were prepared to pay for the pleasures of Sunday with all the chores our father would give us.

After work, we went off to the bridge in front of the tavern and waited for the first of the festive peasants to arrive.

❖

There I stood and looked at the white, sun-drenched houses of the village. The small clay huts were freshly slaked and lined with blue and white trim around the windows and porches. Their sunlit whiteness gleamed out from between the lush green trees and radiated an intimate warmth into my heart.

Just then a stork flew onto a chimney. It fluttered its wide white wings and burst into a long grumbling croak.

A small calf with yellow and white spots stood with its thin stretched legs dug into the earth and its little head to its mother's udders. It relished the double pleasure of sucking its mother's milk and being licked and coddled by her soft, fondling tongue.

A brown dog sat in an open gate with its head nestled between its two front paws. It was calmly watching a line of white ducks, their bulging bellies swinging slowly down the hill to the well.

Two peasants, the sun reflecting off their white tunics, exchanged a few words over a fence. Their voices sounded fresh and palpable in the pure silence of early morning. As they spoke, they left their yards and headed for the tavern.

·:·

In the tavern, the long oak tables were freshly washed and waiting. Everything was clean and festive. The vast earthen floor was swept and sprayed with lovely looping ringlets of water, which one of my older brothers had strewn meticulously with the large tin pump. The brandy bottles stood full and gleaming on the upper shelves and sparkled above the washed glasses and polished lead pint measures that my father arranged on the bar in perfect order, each according to size.

The first two peasants to enter sat down at a table, one facing the other, and ordered brandy. The first one paid and the second one thanked him. After that, the second one paid and the first one thanked. They thanked each other so much that their eyes got cloudy and their tongues went loose. The first one aired his troubles while the second one sighed. And as he sighed, he felt as though they were his own troubles he was sighing over.

Then more peasants began to arrive. Some came in groups, some came separately, and the women followed in the same fashion. The men were outfitted in fresh linen tunics, adorned with embroidered flowers and blossoms around the collars and sleeves. The tunics hung halfway down over their *iţari*, their white fitted trousers, and were bound with red woolen belts, which were decorated with bright yellow spangles and flecked with tiny beads of various colors. The young gentile boys wore black hats with straight wide brims and delicate peacock feathers fixed at the sides.

The women perked their ears trying to hear what the men were discussing. Every so often they'd turn away, seemingly out of modesty or embarrassment, but with such tact that these mysterious men couldn't fail to notice the many forms of dress they wore one atop the other in a mingling of bright and stunning colors. They touched their hair with their combs, they stroked the strings of beads around their necks, and they fondled their sensuous hand-hemmed blouses with the tips of their fingers to ensure that their charm and craft would not escape the masculine eye.

The tables were set. The drinks multiplied. Everyone drank. Everyone sighed.

The quiet conversation of each individual peasant melded together into one great jumbled clamor. The same peasants that at first had spoken so calmly, so quiet and tame, were beginning to feel their oats. As for the lightweights, they'd already lost their wits.

My father stood by the bar and with a piece of chalk he kept a record of the glasses of brandy and bottles of wine that we, the small boys, brought out to the tables. When he figured a peasant had "had enough" he'd have us collect the money before the drunken peasant lost all account.

The peasant girls sat on the surrounding benches and waited for the men to treat them to a drink. They whispered and giggled and it was obvious that they were talking gossip. A drunken peasant staggered over to his wife and thrust her a glass of brandy.

"Here, have a drink."

His wife blushed and buried her face in her hands.

"Go on, don't be embarrassed."

She toyed with him a bit more, and shrugged her shoulders in refusal. The man blinked; he didn't understand.

"You really don't want it?"

"No."

"Honest?"

"Honest."

As the man was about to leave, she snatched the glass from his hand and drained it in one gulp.

The two peasants who had come in first now stood dead drunk in the middle of the tavern. They held each other by the shoulders and drank from each other's glasses, but even this they could barely manage. Their bodies swayed, their hands trembled, and they couldn't seem to get the glasses to each other's mouths. In the end, they opted to drink from their own glasses. They drenched themselves more than they drank, and they continued swaying with their hands on each other's shoulders.

"Mihai," one of them asked. "Where are you?"

"What do you mean? I'm still right here, Alecu."

"Why can't I see your eyes then?"

"What are you talking about? They're right here!"

"Yes, I see them now. But tell me Mihai, why do they seem so sad?"

"Why? Bah, Alecu!"

"Correct, Mihai. Because why shouldn't they seem sad when your heart is forlorn? But why Mihai, why is your heart forlorn?"

"Why? Bah, Alecu!"

"Correct, Mihai. Absolutely correct. Because why shouldn't your heart be forlorn, when for a whole summer you work like an ox, then comes winter and you haven't even got a drop of kerosene!"

"Right, Alecu."

"Yes, Mihai, it seems both right, and not right at all."

Alecu dropped his head to Mihai's chest and burst hoarsely into song:

Frunze verde, empty land,
'Twas not in the cards for me.

Mihai joined in the *doina*:

Frunze verde, fertile land,
May yet be my destiny.

A tall, thin Rom shuffled out from the corner with a fiddle to his chin. A second one followed, this one short and fat, with a *cobză* in his hand. The first one drew his bow over the thin string of the fiddle, and the string quaked and quivered, wept and wailed, and pulled at the peasants' hearts. The second one accompanied him with his wood-bellied *cobză*, strumming the broad strings with his goose feather and humming over the sobs of the fiddle.

The peasants sat bewildered at their tables. From here and there came the echoes of a sad song with woeful words. Those that couldn't sing accompanied the *doina* with a sigh or a sob.

The two drunken peasants standing in the middle of the tavern shuffled off to the corner. There they stood, overwhelmed and sighing:

"Ah, Mihai!"

"Ah, Alecu!"

An excited young peasant jumped up, waving his hands about. "Hey, Gypsy! We've sobbed enough! A *sîrba*!"

The gangling Rom flashed his white teeth and threw his head to the side. The sobs of the *doina* disintegrated into short, energetic notes, and the Rom's fingers jumped like dancing pins over the thin stretched neck of the fiddle. The other Rom buried his head in his wood-bellied *cobză*, strumming frantically with his goose feather—and the young peasant, alone in the middle of the tavern, twisted and twined his feet in a passionate *sîrba*.

The feverish tones of the *sîrba* flew under the long tables, seeking the feet of the drunken peasants and dragging them out to dance. The peasants slowly got up from the tables, laid their hands atop each other's shoulders, and plodded their way into the dance. They worked hard to match the rhythm of the *sîrba*, but their drunken faltering feet wouldn't let them. Soon the women jumped in, fervid and frenzied, and the men's clumsy feet came back to life. The two Roma stood in the middle of the tavern and played with eyes ablaze. The heavy bodies of the drunken peasants became lighter and more limber. They swung and shuffled, they bent and spun, and with their large hobnail boots they tapped out their many joyful steps on the hard clay floor of the tavern.

As the sweet summer ended, then came the rough winter with its frosts and blizzards, which spelled silent, doleful days for our tavern. The peasants sat in their huts warming by the stoves, unable to leave. Very rarely would they come to the tavern, unless their tobacco or kerosene ran out. But even then they would usually send the children. The young peasants of the village would run in, frozen and winded, buy what they needed, and run home again.

We children were also in the tavern very little during the winter. We would mostly sit at home and keep an eye out through the small curtained window of the door. We'd only leave when we heard the clattering of the bell which hung over the outside door, signalling a customer. But even then we wouldn't stay in the tavern for long. We quickly settled with the customer and slipped back into the house again. In the winter it could be hours before seeing the face or hearing the voice of another living soul. We heard the wind that soughed through the chimney, and sometimes the starving howls of the packs of wolves in the woods across from the tavern.

On such days all kinds of terrible thoughts would run through our minds. My mother would pace around, fraught and frantic. She would listen with horror to every rustle from the attic and every creak of the gate. Watching her, we little children would also be stricken by the same fear. In her frightened eyes we saw grim little windows ready to open at any moment and release terrible thieves and bandits with guns in their hands and knives in their belts.

In the wintertime, my father lived in a completely different world. For him, the winter was a delightful respite from a long, laborious summer. He would sit for hours by the stove, stretched out on a cushion, savoring the pages of the novels that had collected over the course of the warm season. And while my mother and we little children languished in fear, my father floated in a wonderful world of crystal palaces and love-struck princesses far from the tavern and from his household. He'd rarely even look at us, save for the moments he was between books. And when he did, he would notice my mother's fearful face and attempt to soothe her with a smile. When the smile didn't work, he would take off his glasses and tell a joke or a funny story.

We children knew that our father was, by nature, not a humorist, and the fact that he had suddenly become so comic only convinced us further that our mother's fear was not in vain. Still, as our mother brightened up a bit, it was easier for us to bear. But as soon as our father re-immersed himself in his books, our mother's eyes turned into those grim little windows again, and again we thought of the thieves and bandits with their guns and knives.

Such fear was our burden every day in the winter, every day, that is, except Sunday. Sunday the peasants could no longer keep away from the tavern. Because for them the tavern was more than a tavern, more than a place to drink and rejoice. The tavern was their village meeting place. They would go there to talk about all the village affairs and, with the help of the tavern keeper, it was there that they would resolve all their doubts and disputes.

The tavern keeper was their friend and confidant. They would turn to him with their quarrels and grievances. They would complain to him about their awful neighbors and spoiled children. They would confer with him about dubious match-makings, distant travels, and business in the city. And to no one else but him could they vent their rage against the village boyar and his servants that oppressed and enslaved them.

The tavern keeper was also the one they went to to explain matters of politics and other lofty affairs, because he read newspapers and had knowledge of such things. He apprised them of the thoughts and considerations of senior government officials, what new laws had been introduced, and even what was heard from the Kaiser in the castle. And when the tavern was informed of some newfangled invention, or simply a bit of news, he would sit down with the peasants and explain everything in a simple manner, with plain examples from their own village life.

Yes, the tavern was more than a tavern. It was the peasant's window to the world. And it was the tavern keeper who revealed to the peasants the wonders of this large and unknown world, and helped them to feel more at home in it.

For that reason, when Sunday came around, the peasants couldn't sit inside their huts anymore, and they had to come to the tavern. On Sunday, even my mother no longer paced around with that worried look in her eyes. And of course on Sunday my father had to part from the world of wonder inside his novels and become a tavern keeper again.

Even so, winter Sundays still weren't quite as cheerful as the ones in summer. Although the tavern was busy, and although the musicians played and there was plenty of commotion, something was missing. What was missing was the summer outside; what was missing was the lovely fragrance of the summer air, and the joyful song and swarm of summer creatures that burst into the tavern through the windows and doors and told of God's beautiful summer world.

In the winter, the splendor of the tavern was one of separation—a lonesome, secluded splendor of a distant people in a far-flung, snowbound tavern.

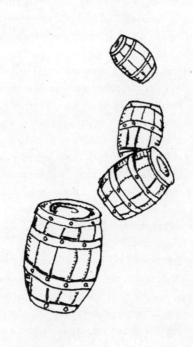

II.

THE CELLAR

In the evenings when my father lit the great brass chandelier, long fearsome shadows shuddered on the wall. The pale light of the chandelier scarcely illuminated the front corner of the tavern, merely doing more to intensify the darkness and gloom of the other corners.

Two peasants sat at a dimly lit table, resting on their elbows and speaking in whispers. Right then, with the darkness haunting, they began to talk of ghosts.

"Take the tavern for instance," one of them said. "You really think there's no ghosts in here?" The second peasant looked around.

"I don't mean right here where we're sitting. I mean down below, in the cellar."

He told him a tale of how years ago, when the cellar was being dug, a hunk of clay fell on a peasant and suffocated him to death, and ever since, each day at nightfall, the ghost of that dead peasant emerges to haunt the cellar in the form of a goat.

The other peasant spat and crossed himself.

.:.

The front part of the cellar was built high and wide with stone walls. That's where the barrels of fresh wine stood, and next to them the smaller barrels of cucumbers and eggplants that my father had pickled. Next to the pickles was an endless array of earthen jars and small pitchers with marinated herring, and the cream and sour milk my mother had prepared. To the left stretched a long cavern lined with barrels of last year's wine. From that cavern split off an even narrower, shallower cavern where you had to stoop to reach the older barrels, and that's where the cellar ended.

But the peasants used to argue that the cellar was actually much larger, because apart from those known places, there were many caverns that had been sealed long ago. They were certain that as soon as they found the first few hidden caverns, countless underground tunnels would be revealed, tunnels that stretched off in every direction, reaching far, far away.

My father would laugh these off as cock-and-bull stories. But the peasants insisted. They would bicker with my father, arguing stubbornly and swearing that they had heard this from their fathers and grandfathers before them.

We little children wanted nothing more than to believe our father. But a mysterious fear compelled us to believe the peasants instead.

Every year after Sukkes came a day when the two outside doors of the cellar were pried wide open. This was the day the cellar was to be filled with the barrels of fresh wine that my father had ordered before winter.

It was a day of celebration in the village. Long before the wagons arrived, the peasants gathered in front of the tavern and waited to receive the barrels of wine. As the coachmen approached, the peasants greeted them with exuberant cheers. Some were so worked up and overjoyed that they threw the hats right off their heads.

The couple of skilled peasants whom my father had hired beforehand quickly set to work. They fed two wooden poles down into the cellar, which they had first lubricated with tallow soap so that the barrels would slide down easier. After that, they jumped up onto the wagon and threw a thick rope around the barrels.

They fixed and fastened the barrels with practiced hands and began unloading them onto the ground. The rest of the peasants looked on with great anticipation. They felt that they too had a stake in the barrels, and therefore they had a right to intervene and advise. But those peasants who dealt with the barrels didn't care for the intervention.

"To hell with your advice," they would say. "We'll handle the barrels. You go find something else to do."

So the rest of the peasants started for the wagon. Everyone, even the old folks and the young peasant boys, found something to do. They brought stones to wedge under the wheels; they fetched water for the horses and fixed bags of oats to their necks, delighting in the fact that they too had a hand in the job.

My father stood to the side, careful not to get involved. He wrote something down in his black book and made his calculations. His instructions would come later, when all the barrels were in the cellar, and we would need to rearrange them according to his plan. My mother stood by him, making sure the little children didn't crawl over to the horses and get tangled in the reins.

The real work came when the first barrel was rolled to the open door of the cellar. Two peasants stood down below shouting up instructions. Above, from both sides of the barrel, stood another two peasants following the orders coming from below. The rest of the peasants formed two long rows, each one grabbing hold of a rope, which stretched all the way to the street. When the barrel began sliding on the soaped poles, the peasants below ordered which rope to let go of and which one to hold on to so that the barrel would slide straight. The two peasants outside repeated the commands, word for word, for the two long rows of peasants holding the ropes.

The further the barrel slid down, the more serious became the expressions of the peasants outside. Their seriousness quickly spread to all the other peasants, even the women and children standing idly by.

The two wooden poles screeched and scraped under the heavy load as the thick ropes stiffened and contracted in the tightly clenched hands of the two rows of peasants. Suddenly a shout was heard from below. It was a wordless cry, but understood by all. The seriousness on the faces of the two rows of peasants had vanished. The rope, which still partly stuck out of the cellar, hung limp and loose. The barrel had landed safely. Everyone sighed with relief and wiped the sweat from their brows.

⁕

Every one of us knew what sort of wine was in that barrel. Even I, the very youngest boy, knew this too. The barrels in the cellar were so familiar to me that even blindfolded I could tell them apart. But this shouldn't surprise anyone. Any boy who had a tavern keeper for a father, and who was sent to the cellar to tap wine, would know this too.

To the untrained eye barrels of the same size might seem the same. But not to me. To me no two barrels were alike. Every barrel was known to me by its seal and by its scent. To me even the taps had their own tell. Each tap could be recognized by its distinctive screech, by its firmness or flaccidity, and by many other signs that only a tavern keeper's son could recount for you.

Yes, with the barrels I felt a friend—but not with the cellar.

⁕

The door that led to the cellar was in the large corridor that divided the building in half. Upon opening the door, you would first enter a dark closet. My father kept all sorts of old things in there—tattered horse collars, broken barrels, worn-out wheels, threadbare beds, pieces of damaged furniture, one thing after another that served no purpose now but might be useful later. When my older brothers wanted to make or fix something, that's where they'd go to find the right board, the proper screws, or the necessary hinges and chains for the job. And so from that mountain of refuse were born the most beautiful cupboards, the most charming little chairs, the loveliest little wagons and sleds that my older brothers would fashion with great diligence and dexterity.

On the eve of winter my father began cleaning a corner of the closet and laying out logs and chopped wood for the ovens. To the right of the closet stood a long ladder that led to the attic, and to the left, the narrow dirt steps down to the cellar.

The darkness of the closet was the first omen of that dreadful cellar. The only ounce of consolation for us children was the flickering flame of a little candle we carried. When I had to go into the cellar, I would hold the candle in one hand and stretch my other hand out in front of me. I would feel the dark void around me and worry that I was about to touch something terrible.

In the daytime going to the cellar was tolerable. Every now and then, a narrow streak of light would make its way through a crack and cast over a barrel or a wall. This made the darkness of the cellar a bit more benign. But at night going into the cellar was pure torture. Because aside from the darkness of the cellar, the darkness from outside and the darkness of the tavern itself were just as terrifying. I knew that in the tavern terrible shadows shuddered on the walls; that in every corner lingered dread and despair. And when I did let myself into the cellar, it seemed that all the terrible shadows and fear-ridden corners were closing in on me.

Telling my father I was scared to go into the cellar at night was not an option. This would mean I was confessing that I was "nothing but a little boy," as my father would say. And this would also mean that I was unfit to ride horses, or travel into the city, or wear tall boots, or enjoy the many other pleasures that I desired greatly and that only a young man had a right to.

So I swallowed my fear and went into the cellar, with a candle in my hand and terror in my heart.

∴

The wine bottles were of all different sizes. There were great bulging bottles of one liter, smaller half-liter ones, and even smaller bottles of one quart. Every bottle had a glass ring at the neck that indicated the correct measure. If we brought over a bottle and the wine didn't reach the ring, the patron would become furious and accuse us of trying to cheat him. And if the wine went above the ring, my father would shout and say we were running him dry. But who could think of the glass ring amid the harrowing darkness of the cellar? As I reached the barrel to tap the wine, I quickly put the bottle underneath and swiftly opened the tap, all the while not shifting my gaze from the darkness that surrounded me. And although the darkness scared me, I felt that if I looked and allowed myself to be afraid, I'd be spared a greater danger.

Because I had to look away from the tap, over time my hearing sharpened to the point that I could tell when I needed to close the tap just from the sound the wine made in the bottle. However, sometimes out of fear I would close the tap too hastily and the wine would splash from the bottle and put out the flame of the candle. To light the candle again would be near impossible. The wick would be soaking wet and the matches, as if out of spite, would never catch. And if a match did happen to catch, my hand would be trembling so badly that in the course of bringing it to the wick, it would go out again.

In this case none of it mattered anymore—not the patron's protests and not my father's outrage. I quickly closed the tap and took off running with the wine spilling from the bottle and, with leaps and lunges, I fled the cellar.

But how could I come to my father with a bottle filled like that? I did as one of the peasant boys, a friend of mine, taught me to do. I stopped in a corridor by the light of a lantern and drank up the extra bit of wine. From the small amount of wine that I would drink in the evenings I would often walk around with flushed cheeks. My mother would feel my forehead and say to my father, "I'm afraid this child has a fever."

The real mystery of my flushed cheeks no one knew, no one except my friend, the boy from the village.

III.

THE ROMA

In the summer, Roma came to our tavern. The large Romani caravans with their round linen roofs came loaded with women and children, with monkeys and parrots, with cats, dogs, chickens, and all sorts of other creatures that the Roma had bought or stolen along the way.

When the caravan stopped, the little Romani children poured out half-naked and covered in filth, running wild through the streets, dancing and prancing around like cheerful chickens bursting out of their cages. Their mothers ran after them, calling them back to the caravan, herding them with their wide, billowing skirts, screaming and cursing, and the children raced around harum scarum, piercing eardrums with their shrill little voices. The fathers shouted at the mothers to silence them and added their own voices to the babble and bedlam. Even the horses by the caravan grew anxious, tossing their necks, perking their ears, neighing and kicking their feet.

Suddenly it all went quiet. A tall, middle-aged Rom with a waxed black mustache and a sparkle earring in his left ear strode out slow and dignified from amid the caravans. He crossed his arms over his chest and gave the crowd a commanding stare. A hushed whisper, like the light rustling of leaves from a sudden breeze, carried from caravan to caravan.

"The *bulibașă*!"

The scattered children silently returned to their caravans and buried themselves behind their mothers' skirts. The fathers, with their fingers to their lips, warned the mothers to be quiet. All the while their chieftain, the *bulibașă*, remained standing with his arms at his chest. When the last rustle receded, he approached my father who was standing in the doorway of the tavern. He took off his hat and gave a courteous bow. My father answered with a smile. The *bulibașă* bowed again and asked my father if he might spend the night with the caravans camped by the tavern.

My father hesitated. He recalled the Roma who had spent a night by the tavern not long ago. Then, too, a handsome *bulibașă* had come and bowed courteously. But the next morning when the Roma left we were missing quite a few hens and geese. The *bulibașă* understood my father's hesitation.

"You have nothing to fear," he said. "My people are honest."

Still, my father hesitated. But when he turned to look at us little children, and saw the pleading in our eyes, he smiled and nodded his head. The *bulibașă* bowed lower this time and ordered the Roma to unhitch the caravans.

⁘

My brother Leyb and I took off running towards the Roma. Our little sister Dvoyre ran after us. We drove her back and warned her that the Roma would steal her away.

"And the Roma won't steal you away?"

We explained to her that Roma only took little children, and because Leyb was well past ten and I would soon be eight, we were considered young men and had nothing to fear.

"*Young men?!*" she scowled and stormed back inside.

Leyb went straight off to the Roma's horses. The horses were big and burly with soft round backs. Leyb stroked them, caressing their beautiful collars with their yellow brass buttons and playing with the colored ribbons braided into their manes.

I stood by the caravan admiring a parrot. With its plumage proudly puffed, it sat in a wire cage swinging on a string. A little Rom ran over and asked, "Want to hear the parrot talk?"

"Yeah!"

"Then bring me a bagel!"

I ran into the tavern and brought him a bagel. The little Rom scarfed the bagel down and turned to the parrot.

"Tell the little prince your name."

The parrot didn't peep.

"Give the little prince your regards."

Still, the parrot was silent. The Rom jumped up onto the caravan and started pestering the parrot. He posed him all sorts of questions, ordered him to repeat words, beat him over the beak, cursed him and coaxed him, but none of it helped. The parrot drew its head back into its feathers in silence. The Rom crawled down from the caravan not knowing what to do. A second Rom petting a monkey at a nearby caravan gave me a wink.

"Want to see the monkey laugh?"

"Yeah!"

"Then bring me a piece of candy."

It wasn't long before the candy was in his mouth. But the other Rom didn't have any luck either. He stood over the lank little monkey and begged it to laugh. He made all sorts of faces, blinked his eyes, wrinkled his nose, stuck out his tongue, but the monkey didn't laugh.

The two Roma felt guilty that the parrot and the monkey were being so stubborn. They looked at each other with sorry eyes, bit their lips, scratched their heads, and threw spiteful glances at the two mute creatures. All of a sudden, as if they'd planned it, they both drew back and smacked their heads together—and with this antic they repaid me for the bagel and the candy.

⁘

The Romani caravans stood on a piece of land to the side of the tavern which was separated from the road by a ditch and a small bridge. That's where the coachmen would camp with their carriages, peasants with their oxcarts, and many others who stopped to stay at the tavern.

There was commotion around the caravans. The Roma unloaded their hammers and anvils, their bellows and tongs, their saws and other tools, and set to work. The hammers echoed off the anvils, saws scraped their sharp steel teeth, sheet metal shuddered and thundered, shimmering in the sun as clouds of sparks scattered into the air. The Roma worked industriously, forging hoops, fashioning horseshoes, hammering copper pans, carving bone combs, weaving sieves, all the while bickering, bantering, and damning each other with the foulest of curses. The women built fires, fanning the flames with their billowing skirts, and put out large pots and kettles to cook. The children jumped around like squirrels, riling up the dogs, chasing the cats, crawling under the caravans, and punctuating the clamor between their parents with their shrill little voices.

When the village peasants discovered that we had Roma camping out, they dropped what they were doing and headed for the tavern. First came the peasant children, breathless with excitement, and their parents came after them with full sacks on their backs and little wickerwork boxes in their arms.

The haggling soon began between the peasants and the Roma, with all the clamor and commotion of a day at the market. The peasants offered the Roma cornmeal, kidney beans, potatoes, and sheep's cheese, and the Roma paid them with their bone combs, brushes, sieves, hammers, pliers, and shears. They argued at length, quarreled and cursed, haggled and settled, then haggled again. The peasants consulted each other in whispered secrecy while testing the Roma's wares. They groomed themselves with the combs, sifted with the sieves, snipped off tufts of their beards and mustaches with the shears to test their sharpness, and when they saw that everything worked like it was supposed to, they relented and agreed to the price.

The Romnija, the Romani women, left their fires with the pots and kettles cooking and pushed their way through the crowd of peasants. They carried decks of cards in their hands and with sweet, submissive smiles invited the peasants to try their luck. The peasant children pulled at their mothers' skirts and tugged at their fathers' sleeves, dragging them over to the fortune tellers.

A hairy old peasant stepped out of the crowd and stroked his mustache. A fortune teller appeared at his side. The fortune teller—a heavyset Romni with tousled hair, a bursting bosom, and scores of beads and silver coins strung around her neck—invited the peasant to have a seat on the ground. She shuffled the cards and laid them out in neat little rows. Several peasants gathered around them, looking with anticipation upon the cards and the Romni. The Romni mumbled something to herself, casting mysterious glances at the cards and at the peasant. She made all kinds of faces, some pleased, some concerned, nodding her head yes and shaking it no as if she were conducting a private conversation between herself and the cards.

"Troubles, troubles . . ."

The peasant nodded somberly.

"And people have done wrong by you . . . Oh, how they've done you wrong!"

The peasant sighed. The Romni shuffled the cards again, and again she laid them out in even rows. Her expression changed abruptly.

"But no longer . . . No longer will trouble lay at your doorstep, no longer will the bad ones hold any sway . . ."

The peasant's face lit up.

"And good fortune will occupy your home . . . and abundance in your fields . . . and you will live to be seventy-nine."

The peasant was beaming from all the good news. He was certain that things would be as the fortune teller told. He placed a coin in her hand and left happily.

Meanwhile, an old hunchbacked Romni with missing teeth and a face like crumpled parchment was roving about, leaning on her cane. She carried a conch shell in her hand and invited the peasants to try their names.

"I'll have a go!" a young peasant called out. "Come here granny."

The old Romni approached with an outstretched hand.

"Give me a coin."

The young peasant dug a coin from his belt and handed it over. The Romni had him whisper his name into the opening of the shell. Then she brought the shell to her ear and called out, "*Vasile!*"

"Nope."

"Here, whisper inside again."

And so the peasant did. The Romni pondered a while, blinked her eyes, and called out again, "*Costache!*"

"No again!"

A peasant woman standing nearby teased and said, "Say your name into her ear and she'll guess it."

This got a laugh from the crowd, and everyone joked about the two new names the peasant had been given. The young peasants celebrated the Romni's failure and danced with joy. The old Romni stood there humiliated. She looked at the young peasant, then at the coin in her hand, not knowing what to do.

"Give the coin back!" someone shouted.

"Give it back! Give it back!"

The Romni was startled and tried to return the coin.

"That won't do!" the young peasant said and shook his head. "You started this, now you must finish it!"

The Romni stood with her hand stretched out and thrust the coin at him, but the peasant didn't want to take it. He yelled at her and threatened her with his hand. Meanwhile the *bulibașă* had been watching from a distance. When he heard the shouting he walked over slowly and bowed politely to the peasant. Then he turned to the Romni and declared, "Witch! You're too old for such things. Back to the caravan!"

This calmed the peasant down and he took back the coin. The old Romni sobbed and hobbled away, hunched over her cane.

⁘

Not far from there, some peasants were causing a commotion around a Rom with a bear. The bear sat on its hind legs with a chain around its neck. The Rom held the chain in one hand and a drum in the other. The crowd swarmed over to the bear. A smaller Rom was making rounds with a hat, asking for coins. When there were no more coins being given, the Rom shoved a sugar cube in the bear's mouth and began to sing:

Dance Martine, raise your feet,
After all, sugar is sweet—
Dihai! Dihai!
But this life, this life's unfair,
As for man, so too for bear—
Dihai! Dihai!

The bear struggled at the chain, growling and grinding its teeth, but the Rom kept singing and banging the drum. All of a sudden the bear propped itself up on its hind legs and began to sway. The crowd called out in amazement:
"It's dancing!"
"Look, it's really dancing!"
Some peasants were so impressed by the bear's dancing that they threw their hats off into the air. The children shrieked and clapped their hands. The bear lumbered back and forth. It went from one foot to the other, spun left and right, bounced, and continued to growl and grind its teeth. The Rom sang louder:

One man laughs, another cries,
A third is stoned to no surprise—
Dihai! Dihai!
Dance, Martine, just like that,
You are lighter than a gnat—
Dihai! Dihai!

The Rom banged the drum one last time and ordered the bear to thank the audience. The bear stretched out on the ground with its feet in the air, rolled over a few times on its back, and in this way it "bowed to the audience."

The performance with the bear had another act that the peasants were all waiting for.

"Who's got an achin' back?" the Rom asked.

A peasant woman volunteered her husband.

"Almost two weeks now since he's been able to stand up straight."

Her husband stood behind her, a short, stubby peasant, bow-backed and sour-faced.

"Send him over!" the Rom said. "I'll have my bear walk over his back and he'll stand up right as rain!"

The peasant woman nudged her husband towards the bear but he pulled away.

"Don't be afraid," said the Rom. "My bear has dainty feet!" At the words "dainty feet" the crowd broke into laughter. The little peasant slunk even further behind his wife. Two young peasants grabbed him by the arms and dragged him over to the bear. The peasant struggled and squirmed, screaming bloody murder as the young peasants stretched him out facedown on the ground and held him by his hands and feet. The Rom covered him with a blanket and slowly led the bear over his back. The peasant screamed and hollered, moaned and whimpered, but moments later he jumped to his feet with perfect posture.

※

In the evening the peasants all went home. The Roma packed their tools away in the caravans and sat down to eat. After eating, they kindled fresh fires. They put the children to bed and one by one they sat down cross-legged around the fires, singing late into the night.

We little children lay in bed unable to fall asleep. All we wanted was to lie there and listen to the joyous Romani songs into the wee hours of the morning. When we got up the Roma had already left. All that remained was the ash where their fires once burned. My father went out into the yard and turned back with a smile.

"What do you know . . . we're missing a few hens and geese again."

IV.

WOLVES

In the early winter mornings when my father opened the tavern, peasants would come from the village to lament the nightly ravages of the wolves. They'd sit fretfully on the tavern's benches, mourning their mangled sheep and mutilated calves and cows. We little children would listen fearfully to their conversation; and at night when my father closed the tavern, we would hurry over to the outside doors to make sure they were bolted fast.

Because of the wolves and the havoc they wrought the village organized a nightly watch. Every night a different peasant was assigned to protect the village. The watchman was stationed in front of the tavern because it was close to the woods where the wolves lived. Dressed in pelts and with a large ox horn slung over his shoulder, the watchman stood at his post all night long, even through the most horrible frosts and blizzards. Every so often he would put the horn to his lips and pierce the air with a long, steady blow intended to frighten the wolves and drive them from the village yards.

But the watchman and his horn made little difference. In the morning when my father opened the tavern, the peasants would come complaining about the wolves again. The horn only helped us little children because at night when we heard the watch-man's horn, we'd feel a little more at ease as we lay in our beds.

⁛

The coachmen and the village merchants who stopped by our tavern in the winter would also complain about the wolves. Sitting at the tables they'd tell all kinds of terrifying stories about how whole packs of wolves had attacked them and how they had miraculously gotten away. Kiva the baker, who used to bring our bread and bagels, also managed a miraculous escape.

Kiva was a small Jew, and not just small, but scrawny. He had tiny blue eyes, a narrow blond mustache, and a thin blond beard that seemed to grow lopsided off his face. Winter, when he came in with his long sheepskin pelt, knee-high boots, and large peaked *cujmă*, he looked both taller and burlier than he really was. Even his reedy, piercing little voice sounded deeper and more robust. But as soon as Kiva shed his heavy winter clothes and sat to warm himself by the stove he was once again the lank little Jew with the small, scrawny body.

The day of the miracle, Kiva arrived with an empty sleigh. When my father asked him what had happened to the bread and bagels, Kiva squeezed his little eyes shut and screeched in his typical reedy voice, "The wolves!"

"I don't understand," my father said. "Since when do wolves eat bread and bagels?"

Kiva shrieked even louder, "I don't mean *that*!"

He shucked his sheepskin pelt, took off his cotton jacket, shed his many vests and undershirts, worn one atop the other, sat down by the stove, and explained the whole thing.

Reproducing Kiva's speech is impossible. He had a way of talk-ing that, if you didn't know him, you'd never be able to under-stand. It was a stampede of words half spit out and half swallowed. But we knew Kiva well and understood him. That is, we understood not what he said but what he meant. We mostly understood from the faces and the gestures he made. So you'll understand why I'm giving you not the words but the essence of Kiva's story.

Kiva had left his shtetl at dawn. It was still dark out. The blizzard from the night before had subsided, leaving behind a deep snowfall that erased any distinction between road and field. For a while Kiva was able to rely on familiar landmarks: the mill outside the shtetl, the house in the field, the telegraph poles. But soon these things vanished too. All that remained was a desolate wasteland, a mysterious void of night and snow. Kiva traveled further but no longer knew where he was headed.

Suddenly a mountain loomed before Kiva's eyes. "How did that mountain get there?" Kiva thought. Clearly he was lost.

Kiva reined in the horses and peered into the strange darkness around him. But he saw nothing. He listened carefully, hoping to discern a voice or a sound, anything to give him a sign. But he heard nothing either. Kiva dropped the reins and put himself completely at the mercy of his horse.

When the horse felt the slack reins he immediately turned back around and followed the very path Kiva had just plowed with his sleigh. A while later, the horse stopped dead in its tracks. Kiva didn't make a move. He sat in the sleigh with his hands shoved between the sleeves of his pelt and waited. Suddenly the horse took off running. It turned right, then left, and soon Kiva saw it was back on track. But Kiva noticed something else too. He noticed, not far from him, the sudden flash of harsh little flares. A fever came over him. He gave a whip of the reins and fled from the flares. But the flares raced after him. Kiva knew very well these weren't flares at all; they were wolves. He wanted to scream, to call for help, but he knew that no one would hear him. He was still far from the village and far from the pasture with its shepherds and dogs.

When the wolves caught up to the sleigh again, Kiva remembered the baked goods. He untied the bag and flung off a loaf of bread. The wolves lunged for the loaf, fought over it a moment, then continued chasing the sleigh. Kiva threw off another loaf of bread and the wolves stopped again. When he saw that the wolves could be fooled, he began hurling one loaf of bread after another in the hope that he could stave the wolves off long enough to reach the village, or at least the pasture.

But then the bag ran out. Kiva had nothing left but the small bag of bagels at his feet. He would have liked at least to have saved the bagels, but when he saw the wolves alongside the sleigh again, he started flinging bagels with both hands. The wolves pounced on the bagels, shoving one another, then growing furious and chasing after the sled once more.

Suddenly Kiva heard dogs barking. And in the same moment he heard himself scream, "Wolves!"

The barking grew louder. Soon Kiva saw the shadows of several shepherds running from the pasture, shouting and brandishing crooks. The dogs' barking and the shepherds' screams merged with the howling of the wolves in a frightful commotion. Kiva's horse thrashed its head, neighed savagely, and sped on with the sleigh. A moment later Kiva looked back to see the shepherds' dogs attacking the wolves, biting them ferociously and wrestling with them in a wild fight to the death.

As Kiva approached the village he could still hear the furor of the dogs and the wolves in the distance but no longer felt in danger. His horse walked slowly uphill accompanied by the steam of its own hot, sweaty body. In the village the occasional candlelit window shed a soft glow over the snow. The small village cottages began to emerge from the murky grayness of early morning and Kiva thought with affection of the peasants who lived in them.

My father listened closely to Kiva's story and never brought up the bread or the bagels again.

⁖

I also had a run-in with some wolves. It was on the way to Iepuren, a neighboring village, where my father had another tavern.

The tavern in Iepuren was run by two of my older brothers, but my father was their supplier. Every week our steward old

Nicolae would saddle the horses and ride off with what goods they needed. But my father didn't trust Nicolae with the liquor. This had been the case since Nicolae had once, on the way to Iepuren, unbunged the barrel and helped himself to the brandy. He stuck a rubber hose inside and sucked until he passed out next to the barrel with the hose hanging out his mouth. From then on, when Nicolae had to deliver a barrel of brandy, my father always sent someone to keep an eye on him.

One time this responsibility fell on me.

My mother prepared me for the trip. She dressed me in two coarse undershirts, over the undershirts a jacket, and over the jacket a sheepskin pelt. Then she put a large *cujmă* on my head and wrapped my neck in a long woolen scarf. She wound the scarf around my neck several times, each time higher and higher, almost all the way up to the cap. When I sat down in the sleigh, she covered my feet with two bags and wrapped a wool blanket around my entire body.

Before we left, my mother examined me one more time and determined that I was not yet properly prepared for the cold. She pulled the *cujmă* lower and drew the blanket up higher, leaving no more than a small peephole for my eyes, which were supposed to watch the barrel and old Nicolae.

Nicolae had worked for us for many years. He was an old man, close to eighty, small in stature, short-sighted, and hard of hearing. He walked hunched over as if carrying a heavy burden on his back. His face was overgrown with such a mass of flowing gray hair you couldn't tell where the beard ended and the mustache began. And since he'd already lost all his teeth, you couldn't see his lips either. While eating or puffing his pipe, his hairy face would crease and crumple like a bread roll being kneaded.

But even though Nicolae was old and bowed, the man could move mountains. He'd saw wood and carry water, sweep the yard and clean the stables, drag barrels to the cellar and bags to the attic. No one ever needed to tell him what to do. He assumed care and responsibility for every task, just like the rest of us.

And precisely because he considered himself one of us, it vexed him greatly that my father sent someone to watch him. Especially after he promised not to bring the rubber hose anymore. But my father, for good reason, kept his own accounts.

We set out for Iepuren early in the morning. The sky was blue and star-studded as though it were the middle of the night. A vibrant moon raced through the sky and played a hurried game of hide-and-seek between two small, translucent clouds left over from the thunderstorm the night before.

Over the roads and the surrounding fields lay a smooth frozen crust of snow, glistening in the moonlight. The air was still and frosty.

Nicolae sat in front, and I sat behind the barrel, bedded on straw. The horse ran at a steady pace accompanied by the tune of the two rows of bells hanging at its neck. The bells jangled jauntily in the sinister stillness of the blues and whites of early morning.

We were already a long way from the tavern. The sleigh rocked from side to side, sweeping its way alongside the mountain that obscured the village. Suddenly the thought struck me: Wolves! I didn't understand where the thought had come from. I reasoned that this was nothing more than fear. I tried to drive the thought from my mind and even scolded myself for being afraid, as I would often do on my winter voyages. Scolding myself always used to help. But this time the fear couldn't be driven away. And as I thought this, I suddenly remembered the little flares I had noticed earlier on the mountain. I quickly looked to the mountain again and saw that this time my fear was not in vain. The flares were glaring from two pairs of wolvish eyes.

"Nicolae!" I whispered quietly, but with great urgency.

Nicolae didn't hear me, so I leaned over the barrel and pulled him by the pelt. He bent an ear to me.

"What is it?"

"I see something."

"What do you see?"

I was afraid to say. The flares were glaring again from the

mountain. I threw myself onto Nicolae and embraced him with both my arms.

"What do you see?" he asked me again.

"Wolves!"

"You're imagining things," he said, whipping the horse.

"I'm not imagining. Look!"

Nicolae put a hand to his forehead and looked towards the mountain.

"I don't see anything."

But when he saw me trembling he stopped the horse and got down from the sleigh. I grabbed him by the hand.

"Where are you going, Nicolae?"

"What do you mean 'where'? To the wolves."

"You're not afraid?"

"Afraid? Eh, my boy, if it's destined, fear won't change anything."

He bound two bundles of straw together and handed it to me, together with a couple of matches.

"You stay here in the sleigh," he said. "At my signal, light the straw and throw it toward the mountain."

Then he grabbed his thick knotted walking stick with its iron knob and headed for the mountain.

I sat in the sleigh with the bundle of straw and the matches clenched in my hands. Nicolae slowly crept up the mountain. His boots sank deep into the snow and left behind great black boreholes. When Nicolae came closer to the wolves, he stretched out face down on the ground. The wolves didn't move. Soon one of them slowly strode over to Nicolae, sniffed his body, and recoiled. Then Nicolae sprung to his feet and headed back down the mountain.

"Nothing to fear," he hollered and settled back into the sleigh.

After we gained some ground, Nicolae turned to me and said, "When wolves aren't hungry, they don't bother."

"And if they *had* been hungry?"

"Oh, my boy, in that case, it's no use."

"But the walking stick?"

"The stick wouldn't've helped."

"And the straw?"

"Neither would the straw."

But we were already far from the wolves. The sleigh slid easily over the sparkling snow, and the bells jangled jauntily.

⁙

One time Nicolae demonstrated tremendous bravery. It was a Sunday. The weather was nice and sunny, but very cold; one of those frosty yet sunny days when the Romanian peasant would look to the sky and cry out, "A sun with teeth!"

In the morning the peasants went to church, and as soon as the priest was finished with his sermon they all headed for the tavern as usual. They sat down at the long oak tables, drank, chatted, and puffed their pipes—a typical Sunday.

Suddenly a boy ran in and said that old Nicolae had come out of the woods with a wolf slung over his shoulder. The peasants left their drinks and went outside. They gathered in front of the tavern and looked on as old Nicolae lumbered along with the wolf on his back.

"What strength!" someone called out.

And another one followed, "Look what the old man can do!"

Old Nicolae came down the narrow path that led from the forest straight to our tavern. His long sheepskin pelt dragged on the ground behind him as he trudged along hunched over, with his thick knotted walking stick in hand and the wolf over his shoulder. When he reached the tavern, he threw the wolf down off his back like a sack of flour.

"There he is," he said, as if he'd been sent to slay it.

He unbuttoned his pelt, took off his *cujmă*, and a hot steam rose up from his body. The peasants stared at the dead wolf lying stretched out at Nicolae's feet. They waited for him to say something, but he didn't say a word. He hoisted himself up by his walking stick, took out a pouch of cheap tobacco, and rolled a cigarette. Then he took a slow, silent drag. The peasants couldn't contain themselves any longer.

"Well, Nicolae?"

"Tell us."

"What happened?"

Nicolae motioned to the wolf, "You're lookin' at it."

The peasants took a look at the wolf again and shrugged their shoulders.

"Nicolae," an old peasant called out. "That can't be the whole story. Tell us what happened."

Nicolae took the cigarette from his mouth, snuffed it between his fingers and said, "There's not much to tell. It's a short story really. I'm walking along the edge of the woods, and suddenly I see the wolf. So naturally I stop, because running would be foolish. A wolf can run faster than a man. The wolf stops too. I think to myself, 'He'll probably hang around a while and eventually back off.' But no, he doesn't budge. So then I think, 'Pity; one of us has to die. The question is, who will it be?'"

Nicolae paused.

"And then?"

"You see what happened," Nicolae said. "I'm standing there leaning on my walking stick thinking, 'How do I bag him?' But then I reconsider, 'What, do I have someplace to be? Let me first see what he has in mind. Maybe he'll back off and save me the trouble.' So I stand there stroking the iron knob of my walking stick. 'A fine stick,' I think to myself."

Nicolae paused again.

"And then?"

"And then it went like this: I watch as the beast closes in. He takes one step, then another, and soon he's standing right in front of me. Then it's clear what I've got to do. I assess the space between us, slowly raise my walking stick, and whomp him right on top of his head. And here he is!"

At those words one of the drunken peasants lost his footing. The peasants had all enjoyed the story, but it didn't make any great impression. And if not for the fact that Nicolae was an old man, they might never have even left the tavern in the first place. They went straight back in and sat down at the tables again.

A moment later, however, there was a new cause for commotion. The village boyar was riding by on his sleigh, and when he saw the dead wolf at Nicolae's feet he stopped and said that if Nicolae would skin the wolf, he would buy the hide. To witness an exchange like that was worth them abandoning their glasses again.

When the peasants came out and saw the boyar, they doffed their *cujmă*s and gathered reverently around the dead wolf. They quietly advised Nicolae on how to skin the wolf while computing just how much Nicolae should get in exchange for the hide.

Nicolae didn't listen to their advice. He took the knife from his belt, sharpened it on his bootleg, and began to flay the wolf. The boyar sat in the sleigh, wrapped in a red woolen cover, and looked on as old Nicolae skinned the pelt. The peasants were eager to help and pleaded for Nicolae to heed their advice, but Nicolae did as he knew how.

When the wolf was half-skinned, the boyar stepped out of his sleigh. He took Nicolae's knife and with the tip of it he raised the half-flayed hide, then smiled back at him. Nicolae was proud that the boyar was pleased with his work. He smiled back and looked contemptuously upon his would-be advisers.

The peasants didn't intervene after that. They were now all in agreement that old Nicolae was a good and practiced skinner.

Nicolae returned to his work with even greater enthusiasm. He turned the wolf over on its side, dug his knee into the snow, and continued skinning. When he was finished, he slowly rolled up the hide, tied it together with string, and presented it to the boyar. The boyar paid him and left.

Nobody knew exactly how much Nicolae got for the hide. But what we did know was that he could afford a drink at the tavern for many weeks after that.

V.

THE FIDDLE

When I turned eight years old and my father asked me what I wanted for my birthday, I almost blurted out "a fiddle!" but then said something else instead. A fiddle was too lofty an expectation for a village boy.

I got my taste for the fiddle from Vintilă, the old village fiddler. Vintilă was no extraordinary musician. In the village they called him "Scraper." But because there were no real musicians around, when you wanted to hear the fiddle you had to go to Vintilă.

Vintilă was a particularly poor peasant, and a lonely one to boot. He had no wife and no children either. He lived in a small ramshackle hut at the edge of the village, all alone. And because of his solitude, he made friends with the fiddle. And that's how Vintilă learned to play.

Vintilă had one eye, and, as fate would have it, he only knew one song. But with that one song he worked wonders. When a peasant wanted to hear a *doina*, Vintilă would cross his legs, wince his empty eye socket, and the tune would break their heart. And if someone fancied a *freylekhs*, Vintilă would cross his legs the other way, play faster with the bow, and the very same song would come out sounding completely different. Under Vintilă's fingers this one song could laugh and cry, frolic and wail, or drag your feet out to dance. He merely needed to cross his legs the proper way, change his expression, and alter his bowing, and the same tune would have a new name and a new sound. And for that they called him "Scraper."

As soon as the peasants had their fill of his playing, they'd forget all about him. They'd sit at their tables eating and drinking, not even noticing that old Vintilă was sitting hunched in a corner with his fiddle under his arm. It was rare they'd ever call him over for a glass of brandy or a piece of bread with herring. But Vintilă didn't complain. He took what he was given and was grateful.

In those moments when Vintilă was sitting alone in the corner, I'd quietly shuffle over to him and admire his fiddle. To me Vintilă was a great musician. In my eyes he was even greater than the real musicians my father would hire from time to time. They certainly couldn't have wrested such a wealth of music from just one song. For that reason it bothered me that they called him "Scraper" and mocked him for having worn the charm from his fingers. Standing near Vintilă I could hardly contain my desire for the fiddle, but I didn't dare say so. But once— and I myself don't know what came over me—I blurted out, "Vintilă, let me hold your fiddle."

Vintilă shook his head.

"No, my boy, one doesn't just hand over his fiddle."

But then he smiled and winked with his empty eye socket.

"But . . . if you bring me a pouch of tobacco, I'll give you the fiddle."

This meant taking a pouch of tobacco without my father knowing. How could I do such a thing! I felt as if I was placed before a great treasure with my hands bound together. But before I knew it, I was standing in front of the case of tobacco. And right at that moment my father happened to be standing there too. I waited for him to turn his back before snatching one of the pouches. My heart was beating out of my chest. I couldn't tell if it was because I had taken the tobacco or because I would soon be holding Vintilă's fiddle in my arms.

Vintilă kept his word. When I brought him the pouch of tobacco, he drew the fiddle out from under his arm and offered it to me. What I experienced next is hard to express. I felt not only that my dream had become a reality but that everything that had once seemed real had turned into a dream. The tavern, the peasants, and the bottles on the tables all seemed distant and alien. Even Vintilă himself seemed different. He reminded me of a story about Elijah the Prophet that my father once told me.

Not to mention the fiddle! It would seem I knew I was holding Vintilă's fiddle in my arms, but I saw no fiddle. I saw a blaze of bright light, a net of scintillating strands that wove together in my hands and wove me right into them. And at the same time I felt as if a stream of sound poured into me and played through every melodic permutation that Vintilă had drawn from that one song.

"What are you standing around for?" I heard Vintilă suddenly ask.

"Give the strings a pluck."

I plucked a string and a soft, warm tone oscillated over the length of the fiddle.

"Now place a finger over a string and pluck again," Vintilă instructed.

I obliged, and this time the sound came out stiff and stifled.

"That's not how you play," Vintilă said, and took the fiddle. When he pressed the fiddle to his neck, a wave of sweet, familiar sounds flowed out from under his fingers.

"Let me try with the bow too," I said.

"No, my boy, one doesn't just hand over his bow."

"Just for a little!" I pleaded

"No, my boy, not even for a little."

But when Vintilă saw the desperation in my face he gave another wink with his empty eye socket.

"But . . . if you were to bring another pouch of tobacco, I would give you the bow."

Of course I brought him another pouch of tobacco. And again, Vintilă kept his word.

Just then a drunken peasant came over with a glass of wine in his hand. The peasant was stewing over a sad song he wanted to hear but couldn't sing. He thrust the glass of wine up to Vintilă's mouth and pleaded, "Drink Vintilă . . . drink and sing me this song."

"Sing?" Vintilă blushed. "Am I supposed to be some sort of singer?"

"Drink Vintilă . . . I'm killing myself trying to sing this song."

"Believe me . . . I don't know how . . . I can't." Vintilă stammered.

"Drink Vintilă, you'll be able to . . . I'm begging you . . ."

Vintilă had no choice. He drank the glass of wine and sang softly:

When I hear the cuckoo sing,
And all the thrushes' voices ring,
Deep inside I feel my heart spring.

"Deep inside I feel my heart spring," the drunken peasant repeated with a sigh. "Keep going Vintilă, keep going." Vintilă sang, though this time his voice was much raspier than before:

I ask the cuckoo to be still,
But through the branches yet he trills,
My swelling grief, it spills, it spills.

Another drunken peasant who heard the song came over singing:

And from a spindling branch nearby,
Resounds a turtledove's reply,
Its melody, black as my life.

The two drunken peasants embraced and Vintilă finished the song:

The cuckoo's song is of despair,
A lonesome tune the solitaire's,
My heart sings both, a perfect pair.

The whole time Vintilă was singing I stood beside the table and studied the secrets of his fiddle. By the time the two drunken peasants left, I was much more familiar with it.

"Well?" Vintilă asked me. "Had enough of the fiddle yet?"

"Never!" I declared.

"That's what I like to hear," Vintilă said. "And because you tell me what I like to hear, I'll make you a little fiddle. Sooner than you know it!"

He instructed me to bring him a thin board, eight small nails, and a spool of thread. I ran out to the yard where there were many boxes scattered about and sought the exact board that Vintilă had requested. From one of the boxes I took out eight nails, and on the way back I ran into the house, opened a drawer of my mother's sewing machine, and snatched a spool of thread.

When I brought all of this to Vintilă, he took the knife from his belt and began carving the fiddle. I stood by him and looked on as he worked. The deeper the knife bit into the wooden board, the more pronounced the features of the fiddle that was being born in his hands. When he finished carving, he hammered the eight nails, four to each side, and stretched the four thread strings over them.

"Now comes the bridge for the strings!" I reminded him.

"Don't worry, you'll get your bridge."

He carved out a small four cornered bridge and laid it underneath the strings. When he tapped each of the four taut strings, four distinct tones rang through the air.

"And now for the bow!" Vintilă said warmly.

He sent me to the stables to pluck a handful of hair from the horse's tail. We had two horses in the stable: the old mare Soră and the young Spirtu. Of course, I went to the mare. But when I brought the hairs back to Vintilă, he recognized them right away and burst out laughing.

"You went to the mare? Foolish boy, the mare's got hardly any hair left!"

He explained to me that a bow must be made from long, strong hair, and only the young Spirtu had hair like that.

I ran back into the stable, though not as eagerly as before. I knew Spirtu was a hot-blooded horse. He'd buck at the slightest movement. But my desire for the fiddle was greater than my fear. I slowly shuffled over to Spirtu and lightly stroked his tail. He stood calmly. This encouraged me. But when I plucked the first hair he bucked his hind legs and kicked my arm.

I'm not quite sure what happened after that, but later, when I came to, I was lying in bed all bandaged up. My mother sat next to me weeping as my father paced around the room.

"Why would you sneak up on the horse like that?" my father asked. I didn't know what he was talking about. I just felt the pain in my arm.

Suddenly I saw Vintilă. He was sitting in the corner with a worried look on his face, holding the carved fiddle in his hand. Then I remembered everything—and burst into tears.

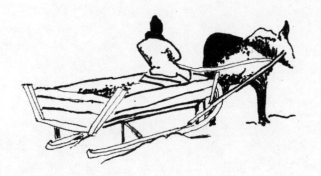

VI.

THE OLD MARE

We little children could never have known exactly how old Soră the mare was. I only remember that when my father and our steward old Nicolae would speak of her they would mention weddings and funerals long since past, and fires, droughts, epidemics, and other happenings far beyond our recall. From this we understood that the poor mare must be very old.

If one of God's creatures deserved mercy, it was that old mare. She looked like a bundle of loose bones shoved into an old dry hide. From the collars that she wore over the course of her long life her hide was so scraped and abraded that whole patches of wounded flesh had begun to emerge. In the heat of summer, huge green horseflies would attack those wounds and cause her terrible pain. The mare endured in every way she could, wrinkling her hide, tossing her head, whipping her tail, but those wretched green horseflies just wouldn't quit.

Her eyes had no real color. They looked like two smoke stained windows sewed into a horse's head. They were always wet with tears, forever bulging from the thick sticky whiteness that surrounded her eyelashes.

And she hardly had any mane at all. The only remnants of her mane were the few stray strands of dry hair which hung down and draped wearily over the nape of her bare neck. At the slightest breeze these few hairs would scatter every which way, like the last few hairs on an old man's balding head.

Soră didn't have a proper horse's back either. Due to a disease in her bones, her back was so flat and wide that a child could straddle her and not feel the slightest crease or coarseness of bone. For us little children who couldn't ride yet, this was a virtue.

The peasants of the village would call her "Mama." The name was well deserved as she was a good and trusty horse. When grazing she didn't need to be hobbled like the other horses. She was so loyal that she wouldn't stray more than a few paces from the house. And she was especially loyal to us children. If a child sat on her and slid off, she'd stand and watch over the child until they came out from underneath her. This I witnessed with my own two eyes.

It was a summer's dawn. At the time I was about eight years old. The old mare was grazing out back behind the house as usual. Nobody was outside. I approached her and stroked her neck. She spun her head around and looked at me for a long while with her dim, yet gentle eyes.

Suddenly I was seized by a desire to ride her—needless to say, without my father knowing. I looked around again and when I saw that nobody was coming, I began scrambling up onto the old mare. But my arms were too short and I couldn't reach her back. I tried jumping the way experienced horsemen do when they hoist themselves up onto a horse. But this didn't help either. With great disappointment I remained standing with my foot in the air. Suddenly I felt a firm thrust under my raised foot. It was old Nicolae. He stood hunched over the ground with a hand at my foot and winked at me with a smile.

"Get up there!"

Good old Nicolae! He understood the heart of a boy. I set my foot on his hand and with a single heave he set me atop the mare. But what good was it? I was stuck there sitting on the mare's broad back, unable to move at all. This was apparently very funny, because Nicolae had burst out laughing.

"Drive her with your heel like a horseman!" Nicolae said, coughing with laughter.

I flailed my feet with all my might, tried to knock the mare's sides with my heels, but it was no use. With the mare's broad, flat back, I'd never be able to reach.

As Nicolae saw me struggling, he said, "Drive her with your hands."

I slapped the mare's sides once, then again, but she didn't budge.

"That was a tickle, not a slap," Nicolae burst out laughing again.

I began slapping the horse with both hands, using everything I had in me. I dug my nails into her, pinched with my fingers, kneaded with my knuckles, but the mare still didn't budge. Nicolae gave her a lash with his riding crop and this time she did move, though just a bit. But at the second lash she surprised us both and bolted. For a while she ran circles around Nicolae, but then she crossed the bridge and started on the road to the village. I was startled, but even more frightened by the mare's sudden burst of vigor. I wanted to grab something to hold on to, but there was nothing to grab. The only thing around me was the mare's broad back with its infinite flatness on which I bounced with my helpless stubs for feet sliding up and down as though I were bouncing on a bed. I already regretted the whole thing and tried to stop the horse, but I couldn't. The more I yelled at her to stop, the faster she ran. I became dizzy and it started to seem like it wasn't the horse that was running but the telegraph poles on the side of the road that were running, and that the fields and the well in the valley were running. Soon I saw the whole village whirling around me. The church came careening with its pointed roof and shimmering cross, and the village houses with their chimneys and their yards, all dancing in the corner of my eye as they chased after me. Out of fear I closed my eyes, and a while later I found myself lying on the ground.

When I opened my eyes, I was underneath the horse. She stood calmly and watched over me. I wanted to crawl out from under her but I couldn't. My leg was hurt and my head was spinning.

My father came running and then my mother right after him, both scared half to death. When my father saw that the horse was standing calmly and I hadn't sustained any serious injuries, he pulled me out from under the mare and gave me "what was coming to me."

·⁖·

For long voyages, such as bringing goods from the city, we wouldn't take the old mare. It was too far a distance. What's more, in the city they would usually load the wagon with all sorts of bags and barrels, rope and heavy ironware, which was not suited for the old mare. For such voyages they'd use the young colt, Spirtu.

This didn't mean the mare didn't earn her keep. She had plenty of work. There wasn't a day she wouldn't be saddled: to bring water from the well or flour from the mill, to take the refuse out from the stables or carry the cut hay from the fields, not to mention the frequent trips to the neighboring villages where my father did business. They'd also saddle the mare if my mother needed to go anywhere. My mother was afraid of traveling any faster than necessary, and with the mare she could be sure she wouldn't. The mare would never hurry. She always trotted at the same measured and deliberate pace, whether on level ground or going uphill. She had a certain reserved stride that no one and nothing could change. A whip of the reins or a swat of the crop made a scant impression on her. She'd perk her ears a bit, flourish her tail, and that would be all.

My older brothers, who traveled with my mother, would mock the mare and say that she trudged like a tortoise.

"She's alright," my mother would say. "She goes quick enough." But there came a time when even my mother noticed that the old mare was slowing down. Of course my mother wouldn't say it outright. She said that the poor girl was very old, very worn, and that we shouldn't work her so hard anymore. My father agreed and it was decided that from then on we'd only use the mare for fetching water from the well.

·⁖·

One winter's day my brother hitched the old mare to the sleigh and went to fetch a barrel of water. The well was in a valley not far from the tavern. The snow outside was crusted and slippery and in certain spots glistened like glass. When my brother filled the barrel and started home, the mare couldn't move the sleigh. She strained with all her might, stretched her neck, lunged forward, but the sleigh didn't budge. My brother struck her with the whip, yelled at her, coaxed her and berated her, but to no avail. The mare tried desperately to haul the sleigh, but she couldn't. My brother pitied her and helped by pushing from behind, but they were only able to go some small part of the way. Once the mare reached the hill before the tavern, my brother's pushing didn't help anymore. The mare lunged up the hill, straining her front legs in an attempt to make some gains, but was unable. She worked every muscle and every vein of her bony body, but the sleigh and the slippery path would always make her slide back down again. She struggled up the hill, sought a stronghold for her old feeble feet, but never found one. Her legs buckled under her. One leg stumbled, then another; she got up, then fell all over again. The horseshoes on her faltering feet etched the ice like a chisel gouging glass. Soon she fell over completely and lay there with her legs buckled under her. She was faint and gasping for air. Steam rose from her sweaty body, and a yellowy foam dribbled from her open mouth.

My brother called for help. Old Nicolae appeared at the gate and when he saw the old mare collapsed he called for my father. Both came running. My father took one look at the mare and puckered his lips with concern. Then he pulled Nicolae off to the side and they whispered to each other for a while. We little children stood at a distance with fear in our hearts. We knew the secrets shared between my father and Nicolae would decide the mare's fate. We were dying to go over to the old mare, embrace her, console her, but we didn't dare. We didn't even dare to cry, though we were choking back tears.

Later, when we brought the mare back home, my father conferred with my mother and my older brothers. This time we snuck over to the door to listen. It was decided that old Nicolae would lead the sick mare off into the woods and put her out of her misery with a bullet from his gun. When we heard this, we began sobbing uncontrollably. Our father came over to the door and shouted at us, "What are you crying about?!"

But when he saw the tears in our eyes he softened.

"Don't cry, children."

Our crying actually seemed to have an effect. Our father decided to wait another day.

When the time came, we children didn't leave the mare's side. We stayed in the stable where she lay sprawled out on the ground, bedded on straw, panting hard. We stroked her, wiped away the sticky slobber that dripped from her mouth, and spoke tender words to her.

Nicolae entered the stable and said with remorse, "It's no use, children . . . no use . . . she's good as gone."

The words "good as gone" cut our hearts to the quick. That evening Nicolae called our father to the stable. Our mother and everyone else in the house followed after. The mare lay with her eyes closed. She was barely breathing. Nicolae raised her eyelids and said to my father, "No sense waiting."

We children broke out crying. Our mother held us close and wiped away our tears.

"Don't cry children . . . it's better that way . . . have mercy on her."

We nodded at our mother's words of consolation, though the tears continued to run down our cheeks. Nicolae went into the village and brought two peasants to help him get the mare up onto the sleigh. She had already become so weak they didn't even need to secure her. She lay sprawled in the sleigh with her head thrown forward and her eyes glazed over.

Nicolae and the other two peasants settled into the sleigh and set out for the forest. Our father and mother stood in the gate and our older brothers stood by the road. We little children ran after the sleigh and when we were halfway to the forest Nicolae turned back and said, "Better go home, children."

We stopped and watched the sleigh as it vanished into the woods.

VII.

CONFECTIONS

We didn't use the tavern's baking oven all week. We only used the stove. That's where my mother would cook our meals and where she would also bring out trays full of cooked and fried fish for the tavern. But when Friday came around, my mother cleaned off the stove, swept the ash with a large goose-wing duster, and ordered the oven to be fired.

This was a job for old Nicolae. He brought in an armful of wood, threw a heap of kindling in the middle of the oven, tossing in several twigs and stems, and the oven burst into life with feral flames. When the wood was all burned up, Nicolae took the poker and shoved the soot into the corner of the oven.

Countless tin platters were laid out on the table across from the oven, some round, and some rectangular, some tall, and some flat, all with the leavened dough that my mother had so skillfully kneaded the day before.

My mother felt the outside of the oven, and from her expression Nicolae understood that it was ready. This was also an indication to Nicolae that it was time to grab the peel and stand by. My mother handed him the trays according to a particular plan, with a particular order. Nicolae placed them on the peel and slipped them into the oven, exactly how my mother instructed. My mother and Nicolae worked together in near silence, almost without speech at all. They understood each other through gestures and facial expressions, through winks and nods.

When the pastries were in the oven, Nicolae moved off to the side and my mother made the final inspection. She bent down to the oven, examining the trays inside and the smoldering soot, and when she saw that everything was in order, she snuffed the oven out with the domed cholent cover, and took a seat on the clay porch nearby, red in the face and weary in the limbs. Meanwhile we little children didn't leave our mother's side. We were waiting for the delicious delicacies that were about to come out of the oven.

Every once in a while one of us would run over, touch the wall, sniff the cholent cover and yell out, "Mama! It's ready!"

And every time our mother would give the same answer, "Ready, shmeady, it's none of your business!"

But our torturous wait was not in vain. We knew that, aside from the other baked goods, our mother had prepared each of us children something of our very own. For one, a little woven challah with three round, heavenly braids; for another, a flat corn pie with nuts and hemp seeds; and for the last, a frosted honey cake or a small tart.

Eventually my mother would look into the oven and smile at Nicolae. This meant the batch was ready. Our excitement was indescribable. We danced around our mother, tugged at her apron, kissed her hands, and nestled into her with such joy and such sheer pressure that she could hardly move at all.

"What are you little vermin swarming around me for?" she shouted.

But we sensed that our mother was in good spirits and her shouts were harmless. And so that she wouldn't force us to leave, we offered to help. We brought the poker, hauled the peel, and even brought her the large white rag which she used to handle the hot trays.

When my mother pulled the first tray from the oven and saw that it was satisfactory, she forgot all about trying to get rid of us children. We set ourselves on either side of her and every time she took out a tray of goodies we received it with fanfare, clapping our hands, licking our lips, and expressing great admiration, which pleased our mother very much.

The trays of fresh confections continued to multiply on the long tables opposite my mother where Nicolae stood, laying them out as she instructed. Through the tavern wafted the warm, delicious scent of cinnamon and caraway, of sugar, poppy seeds, oil, and other delicious spices we didn't know the names of. Beautiful braided white loaves washed with egg were already sitting on the table, along with big bulging breads, honey cakes, tarts, countless biscuits, poppy cakes, and all kinds of cookies.

At the very end our mother took out what we children awaited above all else—the charming little challahs and sweet cakes, the yellow corn pies, and the toasted rolls which she baked specially for us, each one according to their taste, and which we would finally have the pleasure of devouring. Our mother gave us each our own, and although she warned us that we should wait for them to cool off, she didn't explicitly forbid us to eat them right away. A while later, when our mother turned back around, there was nothing to be seen of the sweets save for the few crumbs that had collected for us to lick from our fingers.

"You little vermin!" our mother shouted, but the look on her face suggested it was of no real consequence.

When our mother would begin bringing the baked goods into the house, we'd offer to help again. This meant another cookie or two that our mother would give us for our trouble, not to mention the ones we could snatch along the way without her seeing. Our mother knew our intentions though, and she would have us walk in front so that she could follow and keep an eye on us.

Once the baked goods were in the house, our mother would begin herding us with her apron.

"Vermin, out with you!"

This meant our mother was fixing to hide the biscuits and cookies in a "secure" place. And I have to admit, she always succeeded. It seemed to us that there were no hidden corners left in the house, but somehow my mother always found a new and as yet undiscovered corner of some cabinet or chest where she would conceal these delicacies and protect them from her "little vermin."

⋰

We children were drawn most of all to the cookies. I'm not sure if this was because the cookies were especially delicious, or because they were smaller and therefore easier to conceal in our pockets. I only know we yearned for them. We'd search the house for them by day and dream of them by night.

One time, at night, when I was lying in bed, something caught my eye above the cupboard. Right on top sat a great bowl of cookies, completely exposed, right out in the open. At first I thought I was dreaming. I couldn't believe my mother would be so careless. How could she have left the cookies in such a precarious place, and what's more, such a conspicuous one? But no, it was no dream. The bowl was sitting right there on the cupboard, and the cookies were in plain sight.

Everyone was fast asleep, but my mother would roll over in bed from time to time and let out a moan. I listened to my mother's moans and according to the intervals I calculated how close she was to falling asleep. When she stopped moaning I began scheming how I would get to the cookies. This was not so simple. It required a great deal of planning, and even more caution, as my mother was a light sleeper and the slightest rustle would wake her up. Suddenly I had an idea. I remembered that my older brother Moyshe was supposed to travel to the city to buy goods early in the morning, and he promised to take me with him. This suited my plan perfectly. It meant I could fill my pockets full of cookies and eat them on the way without my mother knowing. This idea encouraged me tremendously. I got out of bed and stole over to the cupboard, set up a chair and grabbed whole handfuls of cookies. I stuffed them inside all of my pockets and lay back down in bed. Lying in bed I could already sense the sweet taste promised by morning.

In the morning, when my brother and I were on the road, I sat anxiously in the wagon, fondling the treasures in my pocket. I couldn't wait for a chance to seize upon them. But this wasn't so easy. My brother was sitting right beside me. It was impossible for me to take a bite without him seeing, and I couldn't have that. With such plunder I needed to be just as careful with my older brother as I'd be with my mother herself.

Then I got an idea. I pointed to a wheel which "seemed to be wobbling" while shoving a cookie into my mouth. But at the first bite my mouth went sour. Immediately I spit out the bitter crumbs and quickly realized what had happened. These weren't real cookies at all, but rather the fermented yeast cakes my mother prepared, which happened to look exactly like real cookies.

Of course, I wanted to rid my pockets of the yeast cakes. But how? How could I make sure my brother wouldn't see? I had another idea. I distracted my brother by pointing out a familiar peasant hut, a drove of cattle, a herd of sheep, all while throwing the yeast cakes from my pockets. As I got rid of the cakes, I breathed a sigh of relief.

As it happened though, good luck wasn't in the cards for me. That afternoon, after we had turned back and were nearing home, my brother suddenly blurted out, "Look at that! A cookie!"

He pointed at the yeast cake, which was lying right in the middle of the road. I thought I might pass out, but mustering my courage I said, "What are you talking about? Just how would a cookie wind up lying in the middle of the road? You're seeing things."

"You think I'm seeing things?" my brother asked and stopped the horse. Luckily, he thought better of getting down from the wagon. He gave a whip of the reins and we traveled on. A while later my brother blurted out, "Look! Another cookie!"

He stopped the horse again and began to get down.

"Where are you going?" I grabbed his arm.

"I'm going to pick up the cookie."

"What do you mean? You're not going to eat a cookie that was lying on the ground are you?"

"Why not? If you wipe it off it's alright."

He got down from the wagon and picked up the yeast cake.

"I'd swear these are mother's cookies," my brother said.

"What are you talking about?" I stammered and felt my blood freeze inside me. "How would mother's cookies get here?"

Then my brother looked further on and hollered, "Look! A whole row of cookies!"

I knew right then I was done for. All the yeast cakes I'd thrown from my pockets that morning lay in the middle of the road, in one long line, one after the other, as though they'd been carefully arranged. My brother figured he'd gather them up and bring them home to our mother. He instructed me to drive the horse and he followed after at the side of the wagon picking the yeast cakes up off the ground.

As he settled into the wagon and tasted one, he soon spit it out and exclaimed, "Yuck! These are Mama's yeast cakes!"

I sat in the wagon like a prisoner awaiting trial and considered the sentence I would receive when we arrived home. As soon as my brother entered the house, he approached our mother with a yeast cake in his hand. But before he could even open his mouth, our mother exclaimed, "Look at that! My yeast cakes!"

When my brother told her where he had found the cakes, she immediately understood what had happened. She sniffed my pockets and said, "What else would you expect? Of course it's him."

I was speechless. With that one sniff of my pockets my pilferage was exposed. I stood pale and frightened, and awaited my sentence. I was sure my mother would soon reach for the rolling pin, or grab the pincers off the stove, or hand me over to my father, which would be even worse. But my mother did nothing of the sort. She wasn't even angry. She just stood there and looked at me. Suddenly she burst out laughing. My father, who wasn't accustomed to hearing my mother laughing so hard, came quickly. After him everyone else in the house came too. My mother told them what had happened, and they all had a good laugh at my expense.

I stood there humiliated, with tears running down my face.

VIII.

THE CURSE

Our Sundays at the tavern, cheerful though they were, would often end in a fight. It would usually break out in the afternoon, when the peasants were dead drunk. If my father suspected a fight, he would have us cart the bottles and glasses off the tables and clear the empty crates and scraps of wood and iron that were lying around the tavern and might be of use to the combatants during their fit of rage.

The fight would start discreetly, almost unnoticed. At one of the tables two drunken peasants would trade curses. This was considered completely normal, so nobody would pay any mind. But soon the two men would jump from their seats and start flailing their arms. From slaps it would escalate to fists, and from fists to sticks. This is when the real fight would begin. Since the sticks were bound to hit another peasant, and insofar as the whole village was kith and kin through varying degrees of familial relation, one would stick up for another, and another for another, and soon the whole village would be mixed up and mired in a full-fledged fight.

My father had a method of suppressing the nightly row. When he saw that it was getting out of hand, he'd order us to extinguish the lamp. In the darkness no one could tell who was hitting who. You could only hear the wild war cries of the beaters and the moans and whimpers of the beaten. And as soon as a son heard the moan of his own father, or a husband recognized the whimper of his wife, the fighting would stop. But these were scuffles. One couldn't stop a great brawl. And it was always a great brawl when Rășcanu was involved.

⁖

Rășcanu was a strapping young peasant, built tall and sturdy. He had big cheekbones and beady eyes. Because of his bravery and fine attire, the villagers called him "Hajduk," referring to the well-dressed bandits and freedom fighters of the Balkans. He wore a large black hat with a wide brim and a long woven tassel at the side. His shirt was embroidered with the loveliest flowers and blossoms, and instead of the more typical woolen belt he wore a wide leather *chimir*, a girdle adorned with yellow spangles and colorful beads. Even his corded money pouch that protruded from his *chimir* was decorated with beautiful beads. But what made him look like a Hajduk more than anything else was the small white sheepskin pelt with yellow leather ribbons and embroidered flowers which he always wore over his shoulder with a chain and buckle at the neck.

In the tavern Rășcanu acted dignified. He loathed the usual chatter and gossip that would take place at the tables. In fact, he didn't like talking much at all. When he entered the tavern, the peasants would move and make room for him at their tables, but Rășcanu would already have his sights set on a corner, and usually one near the musicians. As soon as he sat down, the Romani fiddler would sidle over to him, lean in, and play something just for him. The other Rom, with a *cobză*, would stand at the side strumming along with his goose feather. Rășcanu liked it when they played just for him, especially when they played romances that told about fools in love. He also liked when the musicians sang while they played. At his request, the fiddler would bend closer and sing to him, with eyes closed:

I loved a pair of deep blue eyes,
I love them even to this day,
But yesterday I met a pair
Even lovelier than they.

A while later the *cobzar* joined him, bursting hoarsely into song:

While you eyes from yesterday
Are nothing like that pair of blues,
It's good to be with you a while;
But not forever, me and you.

When Rășcanu had his fill of songs, he'd wave his hand by his ear, and the musicians would slink back to their places.

·:·

Though Rășcanu kept aloof and had an air of self-importance, he was still a good-natured, generous man. He was always willing to lend a hand. If someone needed a wagon of heavy bags unloaded, he was ready to offer his brawny shoulders.

But when Rășcanu got drunk, he was a menace. He'd become a completely different person. By his third glass of brandy he'd completely lose his wits. His jaw would clench shut and his beady eyes would flicker like flaming spears. When that happened, it was dangerous to quibble with him. The merest word could set him off, provoking the greatest of rages. And whenever Rășcanu drunkenly threw himself into a fight, peasants would fall like sheaves and lie there with shattered ribs, missing teeth, and on more than one occasion, cracked skulls.

After a fight like that, Rășcanu would come back to the tavern riddled with guilt and regret. My father would lecture him and he, Rășcanu, would listen to my father's scolding with downcast eyes. He would swear, crossing his heart, that he was a good man, that he didn't mean anyone any harm, and that if it wasn't for the brandy, he never would have laid a finger on anyone.

He would request that the next time he came into the tavern my father should serve him no more than two glasses of brandy. But when Sunday came around and Rășcanu finished his two glasses he'd forget all about his promise and demand more. My father would argue with him, reminding him of his oath, of his crossing his heart, but it never helped. Rășcanu would clench his jaw, shoot fire from his spearlike little eyes, and my father would have no choice. Rășcanu would get drunk again, pick another fight, and wreak his terrible wrath.

Once, when Rășcanu was drunk and fighting, he nearly killed a man. For a while the man teetered between life and death. Word of the incident reached the prefect, and there was talk that if the man died, Rășcanu would be sentenced to life in prison. Fortunately, the man recovered and Rășcanu got off with a slap on the wrist. After the incident, Rășcanu came to the tavern together with two peasants and the village priest. He looked them in the eyes and swore, crossing his heart, that he would never drink more than two glasses of brandy again. He knelt before the priest, kissed his cross, and implored the two peasants he had brought along that if he didn't keep his word, they should break his bones and throw him out of the tavern.

For a time Rășcanu kept his word. When he came into the tavern and finished his second glass of brandy, he would say to my father, "Enough!" then slink over to a corner and not come back up to the bar for the rest of the day. The peasants celebrated Rășcanu's becoming a gentleman.

⁙

A while later, Rășcanu came running into the tavern with news that his wife had borne him a child, his first child. He was overjoyed, and he ordered brandy for everyone. When he finished his second glass, he came to my father with the request that he, my father, should make an exception and allow him another glass of brandy. My father called over the two peasants, the witnesses, and consulted with them. The peasants thought long and hard and came to the conclusion that since Rășcanu had kept his word for quite some time, and since it was a special occasion, they could allow him another glass of brandy just this once.

But after Rășcanu drank his third glass, he wasn't the same Rășcanu anymore. Everything about him changed: his eyes, his face, even his voice. He staggered around the tavern, tripping over his own feet, stumbling into one person after another. After that it was the same old story. He dragged himself over to the bar and demanded more brandy from my father. My father argued with him yet again. He reminded him of the oath that he had given the priest and the two peasants, of how he had kissed the priest's cross, and of the man that he had nearly killed. But Rășcanu denied every single word of it.

"Not true!" he said. "I never gave any oath! I never kissed any cross!"

My father called over the two witnesses again and demanded that they exercise their right. The two peasants looked over, and when they saw Rășcanu's clenched jaw and the fire blazing in his eyes, they went speechless. They started stuttering, shrugging their shoulders, scratching their heads, and in the end they backed out and left the whole matter to my father.

My father stood firm: he would serve no brandy. Rășcanu was enraged.

"Brandy!" he shouted.

My father wouldn't give in.

"Brandy!" Rășcanu struck the table. "I want Brandy!"

The two witnesses ran over and pleaded with him.

"Rășcanu, you shouldn't."

"Rășcanu, you mustn't."

Rășcanu only became more enraged. He grabbed my father by the shoulders and shook him. "Brandy, Jew!"

My father wouldn't give in. Rășcanu gnashed his teeth and slapped my father. The whole tavern went silent—dead silent. It was the first time a peasant had ever struck my father. The drunken villagers went sober from pure astonishment. They stayed seated at their tables, averting their gaze.

My father stood behind the bar, white as a sheet. He looked at the jug of wine that Rășcanu had, in his wild tantrum, knocked over and spilled onto the bar. Rășcanu stood across from him, his head burrowed into his chest. The slap had sobered him as well. He chewed on his mustache, his jaw twitching. He didn't know what to do. My father came out from behind the bar and stood in the middle of the tavern.

"*Gospodari!* Gentlemen!" my father said to the peasants. "For thirty years I have run this tavern, and until today no one has ever laid a hand on me. The hand that struck me today will fall off!"

My father's final words struck fear into the crowd. They all sat frozen, their mouths agape. All over the tavern peasants began crossing themselves.

Rășcanu slunk into a corner to escape the crowd, but everyone's eyes found him, glaring with contempt. Eventually someone took him by the arm and led him out of the tavern.

⁌

Rășcanu didn't come to the tavern anymore. Even the other peasants were ashamed to show their faces for a few days. If they needed something, they sent the children.

One afternoon when only a few peasants were sitting in the tavern, we suddenly heard a howl from outside. Everyone rushed out. A peasant came running out of the woods before the tavern screaming like a mad man. As he came closer, we realized that it was Rășcanu. One of his hands was covered with blood and in the other he was holding a severed finger. He ran straight to the tavern and threw himself at my father's feet.

"Look!" he stammered pitifully, and showed him the severed finger. "Went out to the forest . . . chopping wood . . . look!" The few peasants who were standing nearby looked at Rășcanu's severed finger with terror and crossed themselves. Rășcanu clung to my father's leg with his bloodied hand and pleaded, "Forgive me . . . I'm begging you . . . please forgive me . . ."

My father, clearly unnerved, responded, "I forgive you."

Răşcanu kissed my father's feet and ran home happily, his severed finger in hand.

The whole village couldn't stop talking about my father's curse and how it had come true. They talked about it in their huts and over their fences, in the woods and in the fields while they worked. From our village the remarkable incident traveled the dirt roads through all the neighboring villages and even reached the city.

Everywhere peasants told and retold with every detail the story of how Răşcanu struck my father, how my father cursed him, how Răşcanu went to the forest to chop wood, and how he severed a finger from the very hand that struck my father.

The priest even gave a sermon on it in church.

IX.

THE SNAKE

Old Mihalache was a tiny peasant, a crumb of a man really. If the tavern was full, you couldn't see him at all. But you could always hear his shrill little voice shrieking above the crowd, like the chirping of a bird hidden in a kettle. And this very same Mihalache had a remarkable need to prove his might. It was a need that tormented him and drove him to do the most back-breaking labor. For example, when there was a wagon full of heavy bags to unload, he was the first to hop to it. The peasants handling the bags mocked and ridiculed him, shooing him away from the wagon as one shoos away a stubborn young boy trying to mix among men. But Mihalache refused to step aside. He ran around the wagon, thrust his scrawny shoulders, strained his stubby arms, and seized hold of the bags. And you bet when the peasants finished the job and wiped the sweat from their brows, there was Mihalache standing among them, wiping his face with a big handkerchief.

And for the very same reason, old Mihalache was always looking for a fight—or better yet, spoiling for a fight. But nobody would give him the satisfaction. It was precisely their indifference that got under his skin, and when it did, he'd resort to all manner of provocation. One method involved his cane. He'd tuck it under his armpit with the crook poking out and shuffle around the tavern benches. Every so often his cane would snag one peasant or another, but they'd all pretend not to notice. So Mihalache would try his second method. He'd unfurl his long woolen belt and let it drag along the floor behind him. But the peasants knew what he was trying to do and they avoided the belt. Even the drunken peasants made an effort to steady their wobbling feet.

It would always end the same. Mihalache would wind up standing with his belt unraveled in the middle of the tavern, hurt and humiliated by everyone's indifference.

❧

Nevertheless, everyone loved Mihalache. His persistent posturing and curious antics pleased the tavern. On those Sundays when he didn't come to the tavern, his absence was felt. Such was the case once, when it had been several Sundays since Mihalache had been seen around the tavern. This was not like him. The peasants had begun to worry. There was no one to ask after him because Mihalache had no neighbors or relatives. He tended the sheep of the village boyar and lived alone in a remote woodland hut, far from everyone. But there came a Sunday when the peasants could no longer stand idly by. They sent a boy to find out what had happened to Mihalache. The boy returned with sad news: Mihalache was sick. The news hit everyone hard.

"He's bedridden?" a peasant asked.

"No, not exactly; it's his stomach."

"Is he in pain?"

"Yeah, he's in pain alright."

The peasants asked my father what to do. My father told them to bring Mihalache to the tavern. And with that, two peasants went off to the forest.

In the tavern, Sunday's celebration was just about spoiled. The musicians quit playing and the glasses stood empty on the tables.

My father found the bottle of "Davila drops" and set it on the bar. Both the bottle and the brown tincture it contained were well known to the peasants, because whenever someone in the village had a stomach ache, or just plain felt unwell, they'd always come to my father for Davila drops. The peasants swore by the remedy.

A boy came running in and said they had returned with Mihalache. Everyone went out to greet him. The two peasants held him up by the arms. He was pale and frightened, looking smaller and scrawnier than ever. They led him into the tavern and set him down on a bench by the bar. One of the two peasants that brought him in approached my father and whispered something in his ear.

Mihalache shouted, "It's no secret! I've swallowed a snake!"

The peasants of the tavern stood with their mouths agape. Some of them started crossing themselves. My father approached Mihalache with the bottle of Davila drops in hand.

"Listen here, Mihalache," my father said to him. "That's impossible. A man cannot swallow a snake."

Mihalache shouted again, this time louder, "And yet I've swallowed one!"

"But that simply cannot be," my father tried to explain. "One doesn't just swallow a snake."

Mihalache softened and said, almost pleadingly, "However, I have no less than swallowed one." He motioned to his stomach, "It's in there. I feel it squirming."

My father poured a few Davila drops over a sugar cube and handed it to Mihalache. "Take it, Mihalache. It'll help."

Mihalache chewed the sugar cube and winced as if he'd taken a stiff drink. A little later my father came back over and asked him, "Well, how do you feel now?"

Mihalache blinked. "Better, I think."

The peasants in the tavern were astonished by his swift recovery. They were certain the drops had poisoned the snake, and that it would soon come out the same as everything else a man swallows. A tipsy peasant danced gleefully around the middle of the tavern with a bottle of liquor in his hand. He staggered over to Mihalache and thrust the bottle to his mouth.

"Drink, Mihalache! It'll kill the snake!"

Then the peasant dropped to his knees and spoke directly to Mihalache's stomach. "Snakey, my boy, you're done for! You're gonna croak soon . . . Yes, you'll croak, and Mihalache'll get well again."

The peasants in the tavern insisted that Mihalache tell them how he had swallowed the snake. Mihalache refused.

"Tell us, Mihalache."

The tipsy peasant urged him too, and thrust the bottle to his mouth again. "Drink, Mihalache, then tell us."

When Mihalache caught the scent of brandy, he took a swig from the bottle, once, then twice, wiped the dribble off his mustache, and said, "Very well, I'll tell you. But you must promise to believe me."

"Of course we'll believe you," an old peasant responded.

"Of course, of course," the others chimed in.

The tavern went still. The peasants huddled around Mihalache and waited in anticipation. Even my father leaned in to hear, his elbows against the bar, as Mihalache began his story:

"Well, I was out in the field with the sheep, as usual. As the sheep were grazing I lay down in the grass and, as usual, I played my flute. As I played I drifted off, with the flute still between my lips. And while I slept I dreamt I was wandering the desert. You heard me right, the desert, swear to Christ. The sun was beating down and I was parched. But there was no water. Not a lick of water, swear to Christ. I knew I'd die of thirst. But all of a sudden I saw a brook, like a gift from the heavens . . . no, really—swear to Christ! I fell to the brook and began to slurp. The water cooled me down, it was quite the relief! But in the middle of slurping I awoke to find the tail end of a snake in my mouth. Yes, a real snake, swear to Christ. But it was too late, the snake was already inside. At this very moment it's there in my belly. It's tossing and turning and gnawing at my guts."

The peasants listened closely to Mihalache and exchanged looks of fear and astonishment. Everyone believed that it happened just like Mihalache said it did. Everyone, that is, except my father.

My father handed Mihalache another sugar cube with Davila drops and told him to go home and lie down. The same peasants who brought him into the tavern brought him back home. My father assured the peasants that the drops would help, and the tavern was cheerful once more.

⁚⁚

The next morning Mihalache came into the tavern and complained that the snake had been tossing and turning again. My father gave him the drops and tried to reason with him.

"Mihalache, what's going on with you? How can you fool yourself into thinking such nonsense as a snake in your stomach?"

Mihalache chewed the sugar cube and said nothing. He held his stomach and looked at my father with pleading eyes. And just like that, with his hand at his stomach, he went off to the woods, back to his hut.

Nobody heard from Mihalache for a couple of days. My father was certain that the drops had helped. But then a peasant came and said that Mihalache was in critical condition. He was getting thinner each day and was growing weaker and weaker. My father had to admit he didn't know what to do. He instructed them to wait until the district physician came.

But the peasants didn't want to wait. They went off to a neighboring village and brought an old peasant woman who promised to heal Mihalache. She told him to drink brandy—strong brandy, mixed with pepper. He had to chew up the pepper first, and then wash it down with a shot of brandy. He was to do this for ten days straight. Before she left, the peasant woman warned him, "Remember Mihalache—strong brandy! And don't forget the pepper!"

Mihalache came to the tavern every evening to chew pepper and drink a shot of brandy. But when the ten days came to an end, he hadn't quit complaining about the snake in his stomach. He'd lost his appetite and was thin as a rail.

One evening Mihalache barely managed to drag himself to the tavern. My father poured him a shot of brandy as usual, but Mihalache didn't touch it. He sat on a bench facing my father and moaned.

My father felt sorry for him. He went over and said, "Mihalache, some drops perhaps?"

Mihalache looked at my father with tears in his eyes and said, "No use . . . The snake won't be killed . . ."

⁖

A few days later, several boyars stopped by the tavern. Among them was a military doctor. My father told him about Mihalache and the snake he thought he'd swallowed. The boyars had a good laugh at the story. Nevertheless, they insisted the doctor see Mihalache. The doctor obliged, but with the stipulation that they mustn't laugh. He said that Mihalache had to believe he had truly swallowed a snake; only then could he be helped.

The boyar called over their coachman and sent him along with a peasant to bring Mihalache. Then the doctor laid out his plan. He instructed my father to prepare a large bowl of milk and sent a young boy to find a snake.

Soon the peasants in the village got word that there was a doctor in the tavern who was going to heal Mihalache. They dropped what they were doing and rushed over to the tavern. The women and children came too. The tavern was packed.

The doctor and the boyars sat in a separate room. There, the doctor along with my father and one of my older brothers carefully planned what they were going to do. My father was to bring in the bowl of milk and set it in the middle of the tavern, and my brother was to ready the snake in a small box.

Mihalache arrived in the boyar's droshky. At once gaunt and a sickly shade of yellow, he sat in the back on a soft plush seat. In the pillowy confines of the boyar's droshky he resembled a tallow figurine. Two young peasants took him by the arms and led him inside.

The doctor motioned to a bench in the middle of the tavern. The peasants began to move and push to the walls in order to clear a path. Mihalache sat on the bench next to the doctor, trembling with fear. He held one hand at his belly and crossed himself with the other. The doctor asked him first to calm down, and then to tell him how it was that he had come to swallow the snake. Mihalache told the same story we heard before. The doctor placed a hand on Mihalache's shoulder and said that such things were known to happen, and that just the other day he had to get a snake out of a peasant's stomach.

Mihalache started to cry.

"Why are you crying?" the doctor asked.

"I'm afraid," Mihalache sobbed.

"There's nothing to be afraid of."

"It'll hurt."

"It won't hurt."

And in order to console him further, the doctor told him that the remedy was nothing more than milk. Snakes loved milk, he said, and if the snake smelled milk it would come out of its own accord. Mihalache only had to follow his instructions. He had to be lifted with his feet in the air and his head toward the ground, and so that he wouldn't get nauseous, he'd be blindfolded.

The doctor called over two tall peasants and had them stand at either side. He had my father bring out the bowl of milk. My brother stood next to the doctor with the tiny box concealed behind his back. The doctor blindfolded Mihalache's eyes with a large kerchief and winked at the two peasants. The peasants grabbed Mihalache and soon he was hanging, just as the doctor said, with his feet in the air and his head toward the ground. The doctor shoved his finger down Mihalache's throat and commanded, "Retch, Mihalache!"

Mihalache gagged on the doctor's finger.

"I can't, Doctor."

"You can, Mihalache, you just don't want to."

"I want to, Doctor, I just can't."

The doctor reached further down Mihalache's throat.

"Retch, Mihalache!"

Mihalache vomited.

"Well done, Mihalache," the doctor exclaimed. "Now again."

"I can't anymore, Doctor. Really."

The doctor stuck two fingers down Mihalache's throat.

"You can! You must! Retch, Mihalache!"

Mihalache puked once more.

"Bravo Mihalache!" the doctor shouted, and slyly released the snake into the bowl of milk.

"You've been saved, Mihalache! Here's the snake!"

The two peasants flipped Mihalache back onto his feet and the doctor untied the blindfold. When Mihalache saw the snake in the bowl, he fell to his knees and kissed the doctor's hand.

All the peasants in the tavern crossed themselves.

.⁘.

From that day on Mihalache began to get better. After a while he was the same Mihalache he'd always been. He started coming back to the tavern to prove his might, just like he did before.

X.

SHABBES

My mother ran herself ragged all week. From the crack of dawn until late in the night she dragged herself about on her poor little feet and never stopped working for a moment. Even if she was sick or out of sorts, she cooked and cleaned, sewed and knitted, patched clothes and salvaged old belongings, all the while never taking her eyes off the chickens in the yard and the children in the house.

But when Friday afternoon came around, my mother's work was done. She shut herself away in the "salon," which was only ever occupied when a distinguished guest came or a boyar stopped at the tavern, and there she stayed for several hours. We children knew that whenever my mother was shut away in the salon we mustn't go in there. This wasn't a prohibition on our mother's part but a rule we children imposed upon ourselves, and that we ourselves enforced—first and foremost out of respect for our mother, but also because we sensed she was doing things in there that little children, especially boys, ought not see.

We didn't know exactly what our mother was doing in the salon, but later, when she came out in her white piqué jacket with a gold timepiece pinned to her breast, we knew what this meant—Shabbes!

The smell of our mother's freshly baked Shabbes delicacies filled the house. The white challahs and braided loaves of bread, and the various cookies and biscuits that our mother arranged atop the oven and the sideboard, all imbued the air with the intoxicating aroma of caraway and cinnamon. And through the open door wafted the smell of the freshly polished floor, still drying under the beautiful colored rugs.

Every corner of the tavern had a particular smell on Friday afternoons. Early in the morning, my older brothers would wash the long oak tables, clean the windows, wipe down the bottles of brandy on the shelves, scour the lead pitchers, and then sweep the tavern and spray the clay floor with nice linked ringlets of water. By the time our mother arrived in her white piqué jacket, everything was in order.

For us little children, our mother's piqué jacket meant something else as well. When she emerged in her jacket, timepiece pinned to her breast, she was no longer the foreboding mother she'd been all week long. She looked different in that moment, and felt different too. The wrinkles on her face weren't as noticeable, and she didn't grumble and groan about her aches and pains anymore. This meant we could finally relax around her, perhaps even crack a joke, because while she was wearing that piqué jacket, she didn't yell at us and shoo us away like she normally did.

But more than anything, we looked forward to the moment our mother would retire with us to the clay porch outside, as she did every Friday at the same time. We knew when our mother came out to the porch that she was bringing good things for us—sometimes a piece of halva, sometimes a tasty sweet, and occasionally even a bar of chocolate our father had brought from the city and that our mother had hidden away in some secret hiding place. So as we sat with our mother on the porch we didn't take our eyes off her Shabbes apron. We knew that concealed in the depths of her apron's pockets lay the tasty treasure we were waiting for.

Although our mother knew full well why we were staring, she pretended not to. This was a sort of game for our mother, a game she would replay every Friday. But we enjoyed the game, and even though we were dying for the sweets, we appreciated that our mother prolonged the event and with it our delight.

It was precisely that time of night, and our mother broke into a smile to ask, "What are you looking at?"

We looked away from her apron and tried to act natural.

"What are you looking at?" our mother asked again with a smile. "What are you waiting for?"

Seeing our mother's smile filled our hearts so much that we had no desire for anything else. Ah, our mother's Shabbes smile! How we longed to see it!

All week long our mother was distressed and distracted. The hard toil and bitter agony of her poor rheumatic feet blackened and embittered her expression. She was always moaning and constantly complaining.

In addition to the aches, the pains, and the general drudgery, she'd also complain about us, "the little vermin" who pestered and plagued her. In this case, we'd steer clear of our mother, because if we made too much noise and disturbed her, she'd scream and chase after us with the rolling pin, or the fire poker, or the tongs off the stove.

Of course our mother rarely chased us. But occasionally it would happen that when we warranted punishment she'd do it herself. Then there was always the risk that our father would hear her screaming and decide that her punishment alone would not suffice.

Once, when our mother came after us with the tongs, she pinched a finger and nearly fainted from the pain. Her finger swelled up, and soon her whole hand was throbbing. For a few days after that, our mother was laid up in bed in great agony. Our father was so preoccupied with our mother's suffering that he nearly forgot all about us. Although we got off scot free, it certainly didn't feel like it. Seeing our mother lying there moaning broke our hearts and brought us to the brink of tears.

But how wonderful Shabbes evening was with our mother! She was so different then. You would've thought we had two mothers—one of them for the weekdays, always slaving away, screaming and yelling; and one for Shabbes, a quiet, sweetheart of a mother, smiling and affable. Our little hands, longing and grasping for our mother all week long, could reach out and touch her face at last. We stroked and caressed her, and she didn't stop us either. She even allowed us kisses. And the minute one child gave her a kiss, the other children quickly scrambled to reach her face. The first kiss inspired the desire for a second, and the second for a third, and soon we were all hanging from our mother's neck, relentless with our kisses. Our mother responded with a kiss, a caress, or a pat on the cheek, which was equally affectionate.

·⊹·

Suddenly my mother realized, "Oh, time to light the candles!"

"Don't get up Mama," we pleaded.

"No children, we must light the candles before sundown."

But we knew this didn't have to mean parting from our mother, because our mother loved her children to be near while she lit the candles. Our father just woke from his afternoon nap. He sat by the tavern window dressed in his black Shabbes jacket and a white, ironed shirt with a stiff collar, reading a newspaper. But my father no longer concerned himself with the tavern. From midday Friday through the end of Shabbes the tavern was managed by one of my older brothers. This is not to say my father was entirely observant. He was a man of the enlightenment, what you'd call a *maskil*. He knew foreign languages, had a knowledge of mathematics, read novels, and although was considered a learned Jew, and an "expert" in such things, he was still a bit of a heretic. But for my mother's sake he swallowed his heresy and observed Shabbes properly. Also for my mother's sake he kept an eye on us children so we wouldn't desecrate the Sabbath as much. So, for example, every Friday he told my brother to light the chandelier at the proper time and not to forget to tell old Nicolae to extinguish it later.

But Nicolae didn't need to be told such things. He knew what needed to be done on Shabbes. In the years he worked for us, my mother taught him everything he needed to know about a Jewish household—everything from taking the candlesticks off the table Friday night to snuffing out the lanterns, bringing wood inside on Shabbes morning, and of course, lighting the stove. And old Nicolae knew more than this. He knew the difference between kosher and treyf, between milk and meat meals, between the two types of dishes that mustn't be mixed, and so forth and so on. He even knew about those things a Jewish child was not permitted to do on Shabbes. When a child tried to mount a horse, or sneak into a wagon, or do something else not permitted on Shabbes, old Nicolae would scold us and threaten to tell our mother.

·⊱·

The table at home was set for Shabbes long before sundown. Atop the white embroidered tablecloth were two loaves of challah, also covered with a white cloth, this one decorated with a red bird and two green flowers on either side. On the table stood the two polished silver candlesticks and a bottle of red wine in the middle, glistening next to our father's polished kiddush cup.

When my mother went to light the candles, we stood by her side. The set table, the tidied house, and even the clean Shabbes suits we wore brought out in us the most profound admiration for our mother, since we felt she played the greatest part in it all. We watched as she prepared to light the candles and felt that she was doing something very important, although we didn't understand exactly why. But we did understand that what our mother did belonged to another world that had nothing to do with the tavern, with the peasants, or with the gentiles we played with in the village. Even the two candles, the bottoms of which my mother had melted and stuck into the silver candlesticks, seemed more beautiful and more dignified than all other candles.

Our mother looked at us with soft, gentle eyes, told us to put on our yarmulkes, and with a delicate smile, drew her white silken headscarf over her head and lit the candles as she recited the prayer. Precisely at that moment, my father appeared in the doorway. And when my mother finished lighting the candles and bid "Good Shabbes," it pleased her greatly to hear that along with the reply of her children she also heard the voice of our father reply with a resounding "Good Shabbes."

❖

After lighting the candles, our mother sat down on the big sofa with the little children all around her and waited until our father came in to receive the Sabbath. Our mother looked forward to this all week. This modest Shabbes evening celebration in that remote village tavern was her only desire, her only reward for a week's worth of drudgery, and the only ounce of consolation for the dejudaized lives of her children, who were being raised in a village, among peasants, far from Jews and anything Jewish.

My mother always resented the fact that her children were being raised in a village. She felt that her children were becoming corrupted, that they were assimilating the habits and even the customs of the village peasants, and this vexed her greatly. She worried especially about us little children somehow being contaminated by goyish behaviors. For that reason, she'd always call us back into the house so that we shouldn't mix any more than necessary with the peasants in the tavern or the little gentiles outside.

But of course we were drawn to the tavern. The house was too quiet and gloomy for our taste. We heard nothing but our mother's groans and grumblings. But in the tavern it was always so lively, especially on Sundays when the musicians played and the peasants danced and sang. We'd sneak over to the musicians to marvel at their nimble fingers, to imbibe their joyous songs, and if we were lucky, for the privilege of touching their instruments.

And not only Sundays. The tavern enticed us during the week as well. There was always something going on that we wanted to be there for. Not to mention the little gentile children that would wait for us outside the tavern. We were drawn to them like moths to a flame. And not without reason. They showed us a world of wonders we wouldn't have known about otherwise. They taught us how to shoot birds with a slingshot, how to catch frogs, how to imitate various animals, and many other things we treasured dearly.

But these were the very things our mother detested. Whenever she caught us with the gentiles and saw what we were doing she'd yell, "Goyim! Back inside!"

Of course we ran back into the house, even though our hearts remained outside with those fun-loving gentiles. That's why our mother looked forward to Shabbes so much. She knew that on Shabbes we wouldn't dare do such things. Even the little gentiles didn't dare to call us outside on Shabbes.

Shabbes compensated our mother for all the troubles and vexations she suffered on account of our village life. And when she saw our father dressed for the Sabbath, she looked at him with gratitude. She sat on the sofa and didn't take her eyes off him for a moment. Her face beamed with joy and we children, seeing how happy she was, felt happy too. Our mother wouldn't leave the sofa until our father had finished praying and said "Good Shabbes."

"Good Shabbes!" our mother exclaimed and, at the same time, gave us a little nudge in our sides.

"Good Shabbes!" we cheered in unison.

⋆

When our father made kiddush, the blessing over wine, and let us sip from his glass, our mother told us to say the blessing too. She demanded the same when our father said *hamoytsi*, the blessing over bread, and we dipped pieces of challah in salt. We wanted to oblige our mother, but because we were so disconcerted by how intently she was looking at us, the words of the blessing became so botched and butchered that you couldn't make out what we were saying at all. But our mother didn't care. She was pleased that we made the effort to say the blessings and that she was there to hear the few pious words that would ever come out of our mouths.

Of course, as we sat at the table we little children were mostly just waiting for our mother's delicious Shabbes dishes. We awaited the tasty livers, gizzards, and unlaid eggs our mother would soon be bringing to the table, along with the roasted chicken that she served each one of us according to our taste and particular preference. More than anything, we looked forward to that sweet, buttery Shabbes kugel, made sometimes with noodles and raisins, and sometimes with rice and cinnamon, not to mention the *tzimmes*, the bean or carrot stew which smelled of caramelized honey and seemed to contain every delicious flavor in the world.

In the meantime, though, we enjoyed our mother's gefilte fish, its jellied broth glistening and gleaming in its big deep bowl. And even more than that, we enjoyed watching our father eat the fish head, which our mother had prepared especially for him. We knew a fish head was not given to little children because it had so many bones, which were dangerous, or so our mother warned us. But precisely because only our father was permitted to eat it, we coveted a piece of the "head." So we looked on with greedy eyes as our father licked and smacked his lips, sucking on the fish bones. From time to time a whistle escaped his mouth, and this pleased us very much. Especially at those moments, we envied our father, and the pleasure our mother granted him.

Every time we heard a whistle, our father looked over at us and smiled. We smiled back and practically tore the fish bones from his mouth with our eyes. Our father noticed this, and when our mother left the table for a minute, he slipped us a bone which had already been licked clean and which he gave us not to eat from, but to play with.

Of course, in matters of drawing whistles from fish bones we were greater experts than our father. This pleasure never lasted long, however. The minute our mother heard our whistling she ran in looking horrified and ordered us to spit the bones out. Nevertheless, we were very grateful to our father that he made such a pleasure possible, if only for a few moments.

⁘

On Shabbes everyone slept in. My brother even opened the tavern a bit later than usual. But we little children woke up earlier than everyone else. We couldn't just lie in bed knowing right next to us our Shabbes suits were waiting to be worn, together with the fine polished shoes which fit us so well. And as soon as our mother opened her eyes, we jumped out of our beds and put them on straight away.

Our mother didn't have us children going hungry while our father finished praying. She gave us something to eat and let us go out for a walk. But she told us not to stray too far from the house. We could never help ourselves though, because we'd get it into our heads that the little gentiles ought to see us in our Shabbes suits. But we didn't go too far. As soon as the first kid caught sight of us, we were more than satisfied and turned back home.

Shabbes day was long for us children. Long because we had little to do, and because what we wanted to do was not permitted. But for that matter, Shabbes provided many other pleasures. We spent the whole day with our mother and father, except of course the couple hours they lay down for a nap. But after their midday nap was the best part of all. Our mother and father, who were busy with their separate chores all week long, didn't leave each other's side on Shabbes. They both sat down on the porch outside to while away the hours with us.

Both our mother in her beautiful piqué jacket and our father in his black Shabbes coat and his white, ironed shirt with the stiff collar looked like entirely different people. They looked like a boyar couple visiting the tavern. And we looked like boyar children who had nothing to do with the tavern or the village.

Sitting on the porch, our father loved to tell stories, mostly cheerful and lighthearted ones. We and our mother enjoyed those very much. Our father also told parables and proverbs, but for these we needed to pay close attention.

When our father finished with the stories and parables, our mother gave us a riddle to solve. Our mother didn't have more than two riddles, and although we already knew the answers, she'd nevertheless ask us the same two riddles every Shabbes and revel in our response.

In the evening at *shaleshudes*, or "third meal," our mother always wanted to hear some hymns, or what she called *"zmires,"* but our father was not a singer by nature. We children didn't know what *"zmires"* meant, but hearing that it had something to do with song, we too insisted that our father sing the hymns. But, save for one time, I don't remember my father ever obliging my mother. And even that time my father spoke more than sang, and my mother had to accompany him.

After *shaleshudes*, our mother began watching the sky to see whether any stars had come out yet. We knew she was waiting for the third star. For each star we ran out and quickly ran back in to herald the news of its arrival. When we told our mother of the third star she walked over to the window to see for herself. Then she tapped the window with her fingertip and recited "God of Abraham" to a quiet, melancholy tune.

When our mother bid Shabbes farewell, she was pleased once more to hear, along with her children's reply, our father's voice resound with the words: "A good week!"

For our mother's sake our father ended Shabbes according to custom. After he finished praying he performed *havdole*, the ceremony of separation between Shabbes and the rest of the week. We children also had a role in this ceremony. When our father lit the candles, he always chose one of us to hold them together, merging the two into one single flame. Of course, this rare privilege was also mine from time to time. And even though I savored this moment, I couldn't understand why my father's voice sounded so sad at *havdole*.

When our father said "A good week!" and opened the door, we could hear the voices of the peasants in the tavern again.

How strange and distant their voices sounded to us at that moment.

XI.

THE BULL

It was March, 1907, the time of the Peasants' Revolt in Romania. The peasants were rebelling against the boyars. They took up axes and scythes and stormed the boyars' estates. Swarms of furious peasants flooded the village roads. One mob merged with another, village after village, all armed, all inflamed with the same rage against the boyars who had impoverished and enslaved them.

Priests holding crosses pleaded with them, "Go home! You're bringing a grave misfortune upon yourselves!"

Armed policeman threatened them with loaded guns, "We'll shoot you dead like dogs!"

But the peasants marched on. They brandished their axes and scythes shouting, "Land! We want land!"

The boyars panicked. They pleaded for help from the government. One hundred and forty thousand soldiers were deployed throughout the villages to protect the boyars' estates.

⋅⋅⋅

Our village boyar had a brother-in-law, a captain who supplied him with several hundred soldiers. Some occupied the boyar's courtyard, some stayed in the pastures, and sixty soldiers along with a lieutenant and two low-ranking officers were sent to us, because the building which housed our tavern also belonged to the boyar.

The lieutenant handed my father a notice signed by the boyar. The notice read like a military order: The soldiers were to stay with us until the revolution came to an end. My father was to quarter them. The boyar would provide food.

A second order, signed by the captain and which the lieutenant tacked to the wall, was intended for the soldiers: They must behave in a dignified manner; they mustn't touch anything which belonged to the tavern or the courtyard; and above all—they mustn't fraternize or have any dealings with the village peasants.

Of course my father had to take the soldiers in. But where would he put sixty men? He told the lieutenant that he couldn't give him more than two rooms at most, and that he didn't have more than three beds in each room.

"Not to worry," the lieutenant assured him. "My soldiers don't need beds."

He had my father show him the two rooms. Then he examined the long corridor, which divided the building in half, and said, "There is plenty of room here for forty soldiers. The rest will sleep in the stable and in the attic."

"What'll they sleep on?" my father asked. "I don't have any mattresses or blankets."

The lieutenant assured him once again, "My soldiers don't need mattresses. They can sleep on the ground. And they don't need blankets either. They have their own bedding."

It was enough to reassure my father, but not my mother. For my mother, there remained an insurmountable problem: goyish soldiers in a kosher home! And what's more, on the eve of Passover! The lieutenant noticed my mother's distress. He bowed politely and said that he had strict orders from the captain. One order was to obey the lady of the house.

"But what will they cook in?" my mother asked. "I keep a kosher home. Everything I have is kosher."

The lieutenant bowed again and said he understood. He pointed at the large tin washtub which my mother used to boil the laundry.

"They'll cook their soup in that."

"And meat?"

"They don't need to cook meat. The boyar will provide lambs and they'll roast them outside." The lieutenant merely requested a large iron kettle for cooking *mămăligă*, and some other pots and pans to cook borscht and milk. He didn't need anything else. The soldiers had their own wooden bowls and spoons.

The lieutenant looked at my mother, awaiting her approval. My mother, however, was not at all satisfied. She feared the soldiers would mix the milk and meat cookware. The lieutenant went to great lengths to prove that this wouldn't happen. And in order to assuage my mother's doubts, he assembled his soldiers in a line and executed a strict military drill on the subject of kashruth.

"What is the color of milk?" the lieutenant asked.

"White!" the soldiers answered with a salute.

"And what is the color of meat?"

"Red!"

The lieutenant asked my mother for two ribbons, one white and one red. He tied the ribbons to two pans and said to the soldiers, "Listen carefully now! A pan with a white band is for milk, and a pan with a red band is for meat! Understood?"

"Sir yes sir!" the soldiers replied in unison. The lieutenant smiled at my mother, then turned back to the soldiers.

"Now answer me carefully. What is white for?"

"White is for milk!"

"And what is red for?"

"Red is for meat!"

"And don't forget it!" the lieutenant warned them. "White is for milk and red is for meat! Whoever confuses the kitchenware will face discipline! Understood?"

"Sir yes sir!"

After the drill on kashruth, my mother calmed down a bit. The lieutenant went out into the yard with the soldiers to give them their orders, and my father and mother went inside to discuss the matter. My father said we better get used to the soldiers, because we couldn't know when the revolution would end. Of course this could mean Jewish lives at stake. As it happened, students were already traveling around the villages fomenting hatred for the Jews. They were persuading peasants that it wasn't the boyars who were responsible for the poverty in the villages, but the Jews. The Jews, they said, had stolen this land. My mother didn't say another word about kashruth. She sighed and said, "So be it. Better the pans take the beating."

In the evening, the soldiers gathered straw and made beds on the ground. The lieutenant and his two subordinates, a sergeant and a corporal, took the three beds in the rooms my father arranged for them. The lieutenant reserved one of the rooms as his headquarters. That is to say, during the day it was an office, and at night a group of about ten soldiers slept there on the ground.

When our father closed the tavern and we went off to bed, we thought of the students traveling through the villages and we were relieved that the soldiers were sleeping under the same roof as us.

⁖

In the morning, the tavern looked like a real barracks. The lieutenant and the other two officers drilled the soldiers and gave them orders. The soldiers brought out the straw from their sleeping places, swept the floors, aired out their military bedding, fetched water from the well, sawed and chopped wood, and made a large fire in the middle of the yard. Later, a wagon arrived towed by two horses, full of goods from the boyar. The soldiers bolted for the wagon, lustily seizing hold of the heavy bags of potatoes, onions, beans, cabbage, and cornflour, which the boyar had sent. Shortly thereafter, a second wagon arrived from the boyar's pasture carrying sheep's cheeses, cans of milk and cream, and a slaughtered, skinned lamb. On the fire in the middle of the yard the large tin washtub was already simmering, and two thick iron tripods were standing at either end—a short one for cooking *mămăligă*, and a tall one for roasting lamb. The cooks were hard at work. One tended the soup, another stirred the *mămăligă* with a large lathed stick, and a third was very methodically rotating the sheep over the big blustery fire.

After eating, the soldiers began the rest of their work. They washed the pans, swept the yard, cleaned and greased their guns, polished the yellow brass buttons on their uniforms, and did all they could to please the lieutenant and the officers. In the evening they had free time, but even this had its limits for the soldiers.

They were drawn to the village, where the peasant girls sat out on the porches of their huts in the evenings, singing songs. In the still of the night, the girls' siren songs carried all the way to the tavern and reminded the soldiers of things that had nothing to do with the ruthless boyars or the peasants' revolt. But the soldiers weren't permitted to go into the village. In the evenings they'd sit by the open gate of the courtyard, listening intently, their heads swooning to the wistful songs, and they'd answer from afar with their own *doina*s and songs of romance. This the lieutenant did not forbid them.

Among the soldiers were two musicians. One played the accordion, and the other the panpipes. The accordion-player considered himself something of a virtuoso. If he was asked to play something on the spot, he'd take offense and say that he wasn't some street performer. If he played at all, it had to be a concert. A concert meant the soldiers all had to sit around him looking very serious and not make a sound. The soldiers tried to oblige him. They forced their faces to look earnest and made every effort to control themselves. But as the beautiful, nostalgic songs began to pull and pluck at their heartstrings, they could no longer contain themselves and began to sing along. The singing had a certain charm about it and actually added a lot of flavor to the playing, but still the accordion player would be quite annoyed for a long time afterwards.

These "concerts" were very entertaining for us. In the evenings when the soldiers played and sang, the tavern didn't seem as dark and depressing. But the happiest times were when the soldiers would play tricks on each other. These were simple-minded, primitive pranks, naive village gags and tomfooleries, but they made us laugh nonetheless. One soldier, an awfully fat one with a great sagging belly, demonstrated how he could walk on his hands with his feet in the air. As he walked on his hands across the clay floor of the corridor, his stubby feet flailed and his belly joggled about. Another was an expert at balancing a cane on the tip of his nose. The other soldiers seemed to think it was their job to make him drop the cane. They followed behind him, ran straight at him, tried to startle him, while the soldier tried as hard as he could to maintain the balance of the cane. All the straining brought beads of sweat out on his face and his neck turned scarlet red, but the cane didn't fall. When the soldiers had no other course of action left, someone tripped him with their foot, and the soldier, together with the cane, wound up lying flat on the ground.

But the greatest laughter was to be had from a small, pocky soldier who could "play" *Imnul Regal*, the Royal Anthem, in a particularly undignified manner. He placed his hand under his bare armpit, and with the other hand he squeezed out these strange, gravelly squeals, reminiscent of a certain obscene biological function. The other soldiers stomped along with their feet while simultaneously holding their noses so that one could make no mistake what exactly the squeals were meant to signify.

Two soldiers performed "theater." They dressed up like peasant girls in old women's clothes, which my mother gave them, stuffed their bosoms with rags, adorned themselves with beads and colored bows, and sang a duet in falsetto. The duet told the tale of two girls, one of them rich but ugly, and the other one poor yet beautiful, who were fighting over a bachelor. The soldier who played the part of the wealthy girl wore a crooked, sour expression on his face, befitting an ugly old woman, and sang with aristocratic arrogance:

I want to be the bachelor's wife!
Of oxen, father will give four,
And sheep, he'll offer even more.

The other soldier put his hands on his hips and smiled co-
quettishly, singing with a sweet, charming little voice, as befits a
beautiful young girl:

I want to be the bachelor's wife!
Four oxen are no compromise
For the sparkle in my eyes.
As for the sheep—I couldn't care
Because to me they can't compare.

While the two soldiers sang, the other soldiers clowned
around the way young men do. They winked their eyes, cat-called
the soldiers in drag into their arms, blew kisses, and made ad-
vances with feigned lustful looks and gestures of desperation as
they would for real girls.

And with that the play ended.

∴

Every morning the sergeant would take the soldiers out on a
march. It was a demonstration of military might. The march
continued out to the boyar's estate and back to the village
church. The peasants working in the fields stood with a rake or
shovel in hand, looking in awe at the marching soldiers. As the
soldiers passed the village huts, the peasants removed the *cujmăs*
from their heads.

The peasants of our village were quiet, peaceful people. They
hardly had anything to do with the uprising, although they bore
the yoke of their boyar, same as all the other peasants of the
country. Only the young peasants rebelled. They called together
assemblies in the village and often brought in a speaker from the
city. The speaker would come with his pockets full of leaflets and
pass them out to the peasants. The older peasants were wary of
the assemblies because such village gatherings were prohibited.
But the speaker would explain to them that this prohibition was
unlawful because the constitution guaranteed the freedom of

assembly and the freedom of speech. He also enlightened them about the emancipation and about the land the government had pledged to the peasants over forty years prior, in 1864—a pledge that had never been fulfilled. He said that the peasants would have been liberated from their serfdom and would have had their own plot of land if not for the boyars and the feudal barons who controlled the government.

The older peasants didn't know of such things as constitutions or emancipation. They knew only that the boyar kept them enslaved, that they toiled like oxen, and that after a summer of hard labor they hadn't even a drop of kerosene to show for it. It was enough for the speaker to incite their rage against the boyars. But when the speaker left the village, they grew fearful again and asked the young peasants not to call any more assemblies. The young peasants did not oblige. They went around with the leaflets the speaker had left and distributed them among the peasants, putting them up on fences and courtyards, and calling new assemblies with different speakers. This went on until the soldiers arrived in the village. Once the soldiers arrived, the leaflets vanished from the fences and the courtyards, and the young peasants cowered in their huts.

The soldiers struck fear into the village. The peasants didn't know if they could leave their yards. They rarely came to the tavern and those that came didn't know how to behave. They were afraid to speak even a single word and didn't know whether to sit down or stay standing. The lieutenant made them a speech saying that as long as they remained calm and didn't rebel, they had nothing to fear. They could come to the tavern and pass the time like they always had. The peasants listened to the lieutenant with their *cujmă*s in their hands and humbly nodded their heads.

After that, the peasants came to the tavern more often. But the tavern wasn't the same as before. The soldiers walked around with their guns slung over their shoulders and their bayonets protruding, and the thick stone walls and barred windows of the tavern felt more like those of an armed military fortress.

The peasants sat on the edge of their seats, sipped their brandy, and smoked their pipes, afraid to raise their voices.

And then came unexpected and terrible news. Three villages had risen together in revolt. Thousands of peasants, in the middle of the night, poured out of their huts armed with axes and scythes and bottles of kerosene. The boyars' pastures were set on fire. Granaries, barns, and whole estates vanished in the smoke. Suddenly there was a flash in the sky and the fearsome crash of cannons resounding through the surrounding hills and valleys. Three villages and eleven thousand souls had been wiped off the face of the earth.

And with that the revolt came to an end.

⁖

When the soldiers left, the tavern was the tavern once more. But the village was not the same. The revolt had met its bitter end. The peasants knew for certain now that they wouldn't be getting their freedom, or their land. They sat in their huts, gritting their teeth in disappointment and defeat.

The failed uprising was a godsend for the anti-Semites. The students ran from village to village exploiting the suppressed rage in the peasants' hearts. They repeated yet again the old libel that it wasn't the boyars who were to blame for the peasants' poverty, but the Jews. They incited the peasants against the Jewish leaseholders, tenant farmers, and tavern keepers. Among the students were young anti-Semitic seminarians who incited the peasants supposedly in the name of Christianity. They renewed the generations-old libel that the Jews killed Christ, and since it was the eve of Passover, they also threw in the blood libel, a slanderous lie that Jews bake Christian blood into the Passover matzah. Such a seminarian came to our village as well. He wore black clothes, a black hat with a wide brim, and had a narrow black mustache with a small pointy beard, which lent him the dignified air of a local priest. He went straight to the village notary, an arrogant young peasant who considered himself educated and had a reputation for being a dangerous anti-Semite. The notary was quick to call an assembly, and it lasted a very long time. We found out what the seminarian said the next day, through the mutterings of a drunken peasant.

The peasants sat in the tavern whispering. When my mother or father walked by, they winked and jabbed each other with their elbows. A strange silence reigned over the tavern. If a peasant wanted something, he wouldn't come to the bar like usual. He'd order at a distance and avoid making eye contact with my father.

A short peasant, a lightweight who couldn't hold his liquor, suddenly threw a fit at one of the tables. The other peasants tried to calm him down, but he shook his head, crossed himself, and tore himself from their grasp. Then he jumped up and shouted, "Leave me be! I want to be a good Christian!"

He ran over to my father and banged his fist against the bar. "I want to be a good Christian!"

My father was silent.

"Why don't you say something?" he said, pounding out the rhythm of his words. "I want to be a good Christian!"

My father looked around the tavern. All eyes were lowered. "Settle down, Ştefan," my father said to the drunken peasant. "You *are* a good Christian."

"No!" Ştefan threw his back into it this time. "I'm *not* a good Christian! The seminarian said so." A peasant approached and tried to pull Ştefan away. "Leave me be!" Ştefan tore himself from his grasp. "I want to be a good Christian!"

"Tell me, Ştefan," my father asked him. "Who's not letting you be a good Christian?"

"You!" Ştefan shouted, burning with rage. "You and all the other Jews! That's what the seminarian says!"

My father sensed that Ştefan wasn't the only one who thought so. He sensed this from the expression on everyone's face, and from the whispering and hushed conversation.

He came out from behind the bar and asked, "*Gospodari*, who else agrees with Ştefan?" The peasants looked around and didn't know how to respond.

"They all agree with me!" Ștefan called out. "All of them!"

A peasant approached my father. "Don't listen to Ștefan. He's talking nonsense." Others added, "He's drunk. He doesn't know what he's saying."

Someone grabbed Ștefan and dragged him out of the tavern. Several peasants followed, but the rest remained sitting at the tables. My father didn't ask any more questions.

⁂

From that day on, things started happening. The word *jidan*, or "kike," was often heard in the tavern. Peasants mocked how Jews talked. The boys we used to play with avoided us. Once, as we were walking past the village, they sicked the dogs on us. And when my brother was traveling with a barrel of water from the well, two young peasants ran up and unplugged the tap. Someone untethered our horse, who was grazing by the tavern, and drove it off. We searched for the horse all day long and couldn't find it. Then at sundown the horse came home of its own accord, the untied rope dangling down to its feet.

Yes, the tavern certainly wasn't the same. My mother let a few words slip about sending the little children to board somewhere in the city. But my father disagreed. He said we mustn't show that we had something to fear. My mother paced around the house worried, always keeping the little children close by.

Three peasants came into the tavern with a strange look in their eyes. My father went behind the bar, but the peasants didn't order anything. They sat on the bench facing my father, their hands resting on their canes, in silence. They smoked and stared.

My father asked, "Something to say, *Gospodari*?"

One got up and twirled his mustache.

"We are a delegation . . . the village sent us . . ."

The peasant could say nothing more. He shrugged his shoulders and sat back down again.

Another one got up. "Yes, we are a delegation. We came to ask you to forgive Ștefan's blathering. But . . ."

"But what?" My father asked.

This peasant was also at a loss for words.

"Well, the thing is . . ." the third peasant got up and mustered the words. "Ştefan was talking nonsense . . . a drunkard will do that . . . but . . . he did mean something . . . obviously, this need not be said . . . but we must talk it out like adults . . . we came . . . that is to say, the village sent us . . ."

"Don't mince words," my father said.

"Well, as you know . . . we are a delegation. We came to ask you something . . ."

"Ask."

"The thing is . . . actually it's about him, the seminarian . . . he says we aren't good Christians . . . you are educated . . . you read novels and gazettes . . . we want you to tell us—what does it mean to be a good Christian?"

"You have a priest, don't you?" my father said. "Why don't you ask your priest?"

"We asked him . . . of course . . . but the priest says one thing and the seminarian says something else."

"A good Christian must obey his priest," my father said.

"Correct . . . absolutely . . . but he, the seminarian . . . he says that because of the Jews we can't be good Christians . . . He says that they've expelled the Jews from other villages . . . he says we should do the same . . . But we don't have any Jews . . ."

"What do you mean you don't have any? *I* am a Jew."

"God forbid!" The peasant crossed himself. "You . . . you're not a Jew . . . I mean . . . yes . . . a Jew . . . but you're different . . ."

"I'm no different. I'm a Jew like any other Jew."

"What are you talking about? You're Herşcu . . . *our* Herşcu . . ."

The three peasants motioned to each other and headed for the door. At the door the last peasant turned around and repeated, "God forbid!"

Distressing news arrived from the surrounding villages. In one village, the peasants attacked a Jewish merchant, dragged him out of his wagon, beat him black and blue, and left him lying bloody in the middle of the road. In another village the peasants organized a pogrom against a Jewish tavern. They broke windows, smashed tables and chairs, and pillaged what remained.

In the cities students held demonstrations. They marched through the streets carrying clubs and placards and singing anti-Semitic songs. On the placards were painted caricatures of old Jews with vile captions. One placard depicted a Christian grinding a Jew with a meat grinder as a wurst labeled "kosher" came out the other side.

There was unrest in our village as well. The young peasants asked their fathers to obey the seminarians and act like "good Christians." Things started happening at the tavern too. Once, when my father handed a peasant a bottle of wine, the peasant "accidentally" tipped it over, spilling wine all over the table. My father pretended not to notice. He wiped off the table and handed the peasant another bottle of wine. A boy stuck his foot out when my brother was walking by, only to feign surprise when my brother fell down.

My mother brought up sending the little children away for a second time. But even after everything, my father disagreed. He decided to speak openly with the peasants of the village. My mother pleaded with him not to do that. But my father had made his decision.

⁙

It was Sunday morning, just as the peasants were coming out of church. At my father's request, everyone came to the tavern. Even mothers with little children came. The tavern was packed and many peasants had to stand outside.

My father stood behind the bar, pale as a ghost. My mother cowered in the house, peering out through the curtained window of the door. It was silent in the tavern. The peasants waited for my father to speak. My father said he wished to speak with all the peasants and, because there was not a place for everyone in the tavern, they should all go outside into the yard. He came out from behind the bar and the peasants followed him.

In the yard, my father hoisted himself up on a barrel facing the peasants.

"Gospodari!" my father said. "I know full well what's been going on in the village. I also know what the seminarians have told you. I'm the only Jew living among you here in the village. I am one, and you are many. You can do with me what you wish."

"God forbid!" someone shouted.

"Listen, *Gospodari!*" my father continued. "Not long ago there was an uprising. The uprising was against the boyars. But students traveled through the villages trying to persuade peasants that the Jews had stolen this land. I ask you, *Gospodari*— does that sound right to you? You know full well that Jews are not permitted to own land. So how can Jews steal that which they cannot own?"

A peasant called out, "But they do have taverns!"

"Yes," my father said. "They do have taverns; but only in cities."

"But you have a tavern right here in the village!"

"True," my father said. "I have a tavern in the village. But do you know why I am permitted to have a tavern in the village?"

A peasant jumped up on another barrel, *"Gospodari!* I'll tell you why. But you must answer my questions. Remember the war with the Turks?"

"We remember."

"Remember the battle at Plevna?"

"We remember."

"So know this: our Herşcu was there at Plevna! Yes, at Plevna! He went into battle and captured Plevna! For that he was permitted to have a tavern in the village."

The peasant's speech made quite an impression, though not on everyone. Some were stubborn.

My father addressed them again:

"Hear me out, *Gospodari*! I've run the tavern here for thirty years. My children have been raised together with yours. Served in the military together. We've been through a lot, good times and bad. In the bad times, I've always been a friend to you."

My father noticed a few peasants fuming.

"Zamfirescu!" he called to one of them. "I see you stewing over there. Let me ask you, do you remember when your first child was born? Already twenty years ago now. Who gave you the money to baptize your child? I did! Tell me, Zamfirescu, did you ever repay me that favor?"

Zamfirescu looked down in shame.

My father asked another, "And you Moraru! Who helped you marry off your daughter? I helped you! It's already been eight years since they got married. Tell me, Moraru, have you ever repaid me?"

And Moraru looked down in shame.

"And you Ionescu!" my father turned to yet another. "Remember when your wife passed away? Her body was lying there in the house and you didn't have any money to have her buried. Who did you come to? To me! Tell me, Ionescu, did you ever repay me?"

Ionescu was speechless.

"*Gospodari!*" my father turned to face the crowd. "I do not demand to be repaid. I merely ask you, am I not right when I say that I've always been a friend to you?"

"Right!"

A club was brandished above the crowd.

"He may be right, but he's still a Jew!"

The oldest peasant in the village, a man close to ninety years old with a head of white hair, slowly made his way through the crowd, leaning on a cane. He stood by my father, facing the peasants, and said, "*Gospodari*! Let me tell you what Herșcu has done for us."

The courtyard was silent. None but a few young peasants protested. The peasant spoke firmly, but calmly.

"This is a story dating back nearly thirty years. You young bucks grumbling over there, you wouldn't remember this. At that time you weren't even in your mother's belly. So listen close. The village was full of cattle. Every household had a cow. But there was not a single bull. We used to bring the cows to other villages where there were bulls. But we couldn't keep this up. Respectable people don't behave this way. So we came to Herşcu. 'Herşcu,' we said. 'This isn't working. A village full of cattle, and not a single bull. What can we do? We need a bull.' Herşcu listened to us and said, 'Yes, we need a bull.' 'Right Herşcu,' we said. 'We definitely need a bull. But a bull costs money, and our village is poor.' Herşcu thought for a moment. Then he exclaimed, 'I'm buying you a bull!' And that's what Herşcu did. Our Herşcu here."

The old man's speech made a great impression on the peasants. The words "Our Herşcu!" rang out from all around.

The young peasants had quit their grumbling. The old man shook Herşcu's hand, and after him other peasants did so as well.

My father winked at my older brother. My brother knew exactly what my father was thinking. He ran into the tavern and brought out a bottle of brandy. Old Nicolae carried a tray of glasses behind him.

My father poured the glasses and said, "Drink, *Gospodari*!"

The peasants lunged for the glasses. They held them in the air and toasted my father.

"Long live our Herşcu!"

My brother brought out a second and a third bottle of brandy. The oldest peasant insisted that my father should drink a toast with the entire village. My father took a glass in hand and said, "L'chaim, *Gospodari*!"

"Long live our Herşcu!" the peasants responded.

One of the men from the delegation who had come into the tavern not long ago jumped up onto the barrel and called out to the peasants, "Listen here, *Gospodari*! You know what's been happening all over this country. The students and the seminarians have gotten everyone all worked up. The villages are enraged. Our Herșcu here lives alone right along the road, far from the village. All kinds of people travel right past here. As the Romanian saying goes, you never know whence the hare will spring. Let us assign two guards, one by day and one by night, to protect our Herșcu! All agreed?"

"Agreed!"

The peasants rejoiced. They'd had enough brandy to become cheerful, but not drunk. The mothers and the little children went back home. The other peasants went into the tavern, where the musicians my father had arranged for were waiting for them.

That Sunday was a joyous one at the tavern.

⁘

But soon a messenger on horseback brought terrible news. He said that on his way he had run into a mob of angry peasants who were going into the city to settle the score with the Jews. The road to the city led right past our tavern. My father was worried. My mother insisted that he close the tavern and that we hide out in the village. My father said it wouldn't help. If the peasants wanted to buy something and saw that a Jew had closed the tavern, it'd be even worse. The guard that was assigned to the tavern agreed with my father. He said he'd go inform the village. My father told him to take our horse since it'd be quicker.

We stood on the bridge before the tavern and watched as the guard rode through the village. Peasants began running from house to house and courtyard to courtyard. Those that ran ahead waved along the others that came after them. The road from the village to the tavern was flooded with men and women both young and old, all armed with clubs, shovels, rakes, scythes, and flat wooden boards.

The peasants called for the tavern to be closed and promptly encircled the building. In about a half an hour, the mob showed up. When they approached the tavern and noticed the village peasants were armed, they assumed that here too an attack on the Jews was also in the offing. They greeted the village peasants with cheers of brotherhood and anti-Semitic epithets.

But when they noticed that the village peasants weren't answering their cheers, they were completely astonished.

"What's going on here?" they asked.

The old man, who had spoken in the courtyard just a few days ago, approached the mob and said, "Nothing's going on here, and nothing will!"

"The Jew paid you off!" a stranger called out.

"No one needed to pay us off," the old man said. "But if you would like to buy something, you can be so kind as to go over to that window there." He indicated a side window of the tavern. "There someone will give you what you need. But I urge you as a brother—buy what you need and be on your way."

The strangers stood speechless. They looked at each other for a while, not knowing what to do. Then, one by one, they formed a line at the window. Two village peasants stood there and took their orders. First they asked for the money and then they told my father through the window what to serve them. When one of the strangers had gotten what he needed, the two peasants led him away from the window and the peasants of our village, who were standing in rows on either side, guided him with sticks and shovels to the road.

Once the whole mob was standing in the road the old man went back and said, "Now be on your way, and God be with you. But again, I urge you as a brother—don't go where the devil leads you!"

And with that, the strangers went on their way.

XII.

MY FATHER'S
PROVERBS

INTRODUCTION

My father would refrain from hitting his children. However, children are children, after all, and a father must be a father.

But one time my father punished me for a crime I had not committed. My sister, the youngest, was guilty. But the youngest child tends to be more often believed by their father, so I caught the beating.

While my father held me on his knee and spanked me with a switch, I screamed, not so much from the pain, but from the injustice of it all.

"Papa!" I shouted. "Where's the justice?"

The word "justice" coming out of the mouth of an eight-year-old boy apparently made an impression on my father. He let me down from his knee and said, suppressing a smile, "You'll go to your grave with your justice."

Since then half a century has gone by, and my father is still right. But I'll be damned if I regret it. My only regret is that I didn't yet know how to tell my father that this sense of justice I inherited from no other but him.

Needless to say, my father was a poor man. Poor, yes, but not a beggar. The difference between the two I learned from him. "A poor man," my father said, "is just an unfortunate soul without a penny. And a beggar is someone whose soul's not worth a penny to begin with." He also used to say, "It's miserable to be a poor man, but it's shameful to be a beggar." Such proverbs I heard often from my father. A few of them I remember precisely as he said them, and a few I remember by their meaning, according to the influence they had on me.

To this day my father's proverbs accompany me like a light upon my path. It is the finest inheritance he left me. But such an inheritance belongs not only to the inheritor. Therefore I give you my father's proverbs. May they be a gift given to the world by a Jewish tavern keeper from Romania, through the writings of his son.

1

A Christian asked my father, "Do you think that all Christians are bad and all Jews are good?"

"God forbid!" my father said. "It's simply that a Jew is bad when he is not good, and a Christian is good when he is not bad."

2

Another Christian once asked my father, "How come Jews are always talking with their hands? We Christians don't talk with our hands."

"This is true," my father said. "We use our hands for talking, and you use them for hitting."

3

A Jew lamented to my father, "Oy, Hersh, where in the world does one find the truth?"

My father said to him, "Well who told you to lose it in the first place?"

4

My father didn't believe in bargains. Once, my mother showed him something she bought in the city. "What do you say, Hersh? Quite a bargain, don't you think?"

"I don't know," my father said. "To me it's a bargain when you pay the right price for the right thing."

5

When my father heard a well-known proverb, he'd often add his own commentary. To the saying, "You gotta walk a mile in someone else's shoes before you know whose feet are aching," my father would add: "Not true, because those with aching feet are sure to let everybody know about it."

6

To the saying, "Tell me who your friends are, I'll tell you who you are," my father would add: "Actually it's quite the opposite. Tell me who your enemies are and I'll tell you who you are, because a friend you can sometimes have by accident, but an enemy is always for a reason."

7

If someone was in a real hurry, my father would say, "Those that rush may very well arrive quicker, but rarely in the right place."

8

A Jew asked my father, "What's going on, Hersh, how's it going?"

My father said, "It's going how it should be. I'm becoming a little more accustomed to my troubles and they're becoming a little more accustomed to me."

9

We had a relative in the family who had the reputation of being a lousy homemaker, a real slob. Her house was always full of clutter. My mother would try and stick up for her, "I don't know what you want from her. She's always busy, always cleaning." But my father would say, "A good homemaker is not one who cleans, but one who doesn't make a mess in the first place."

10

A Jew was complaining to my father that he was having marital troubles. His wife wouldn't do as he said. My father gave him this piece of advice: "If you want your wife to follow your lead, you must lead from behind."

11

A merchant confessed to my father, "I'll tell you something, business is a swindle."

"True," my father said, "but a businessman who knows that is an honest man."

12

My father had a nice parable for explaining mistakes. "Mistakes are like buttons on a jacket. If you skip the first button, the rest of the buttons will all go crooked. Then you'll notice a hole without a button at the bottom. When you look for the button underneath, you'll be surprised when it's not there. With a mistake it's just the same. When you make a mistake you don't even realize it, then later you're surprised to find the trouble you've caused."

13

A certain Jew with a tendency to talk to himself would often come to the tavern during his travels. My father didn't want to embarrass him, so he pretended not to hear. Another Jew, also a passerby, noticed this and remarked to my father, "How do you like this guy? He's talking to himself like a crazy person."

My father said to him, "Every person has two tongues: with one he talks to others, and with the other he talks to himself."

14

A village merchant used to board with us. He was an incredibly poor man, not to mention faint-hearted, but a very honest Jew. He complained to my father that people gave him a hard time, and that they cursed at him.

"How come this happens to me Hersh?" The Jew contended, "I swear I don't deserve it."

"I believe you," my father said. "But the best indication that a man doesn't deserve ridicule is that it doesn't bother him."

15

Once, on Shabbes, I was wearing a new shirt and stained it almost immediately after putting it on. My mother shouted, "Worn once and it's soiled already!"

I tried to defend myself, "It's just one stain, Mama."

My father overheard this and said, "Wipe it off young man. If you don't wipe off the first stain you won't even notice the second."

16

Someone asked my father once, "What do you do about a liar?"

"With a liar you do two things," my father said. "First you take pity on him, then you watch out for him."

17

A peasant complained, "I look so strong, and my wife, so small and weak, yet she leads me by the nose. Where does she find the strength?"

My father said, "A woman's strength stems from her weakness."

18

A peasant came to ask my father for advice. He was terribly upset. My father told him to wait until morning. "I need advice now, not tomorrow," the peasant contended.

"Do as I say," my father said.

"But what difference will tomorrow make?"

"Well, as you said, tomorrow you might not need the advice anymore."

19

One time the question was raised whether one needs to tell a liar that he's lying. "It's a waste of words," my father said. "Because if he really heard what you were saying, he wouldn't be what he was in the first place."

20

A peasant boasted that he always told the truth. My father gave him the following advice: "Listen to me, don't ever say that. After hearing that, no one will believe you tell the truth even some of the time."

21

My mother was a very hospitable woman. But if a guest were to come over, she wouldn't quite know what to do. She was always making a fuss over them. One time, my father noticed that a guest was uncomfortable with all my mother's attention. When the guest left, my father said to my mother, "The idea isn't to overwhelm the guest, just to give them what they need and leave them be."

22

Once, my father traveled to the city and brought me with him. In the city we went to a restaurant and my father ordered food. The food wasn't to his liking. Aside from that, the table was clearly very dirty. Before leaving, my father called over the waiter and asked him, "Is the owner here?"

"No," the waiter answered. "Did you need to see him for something?" "Yes," my father said. "I wanted to give him a kiss goodbye, since I won't be seeing him anymore."

23

In a nearby shtetl a *magid*, a traveling Jewish preacher, gave a sermon. Later on, the Jews of that shtetl were walking by our tavern and couldn't say enough good things about how clever the *magid*'s sermon was. One Jew expressed regret that my father hadn't gotten to hear the *magid*. "A shame, Hersh, that you didn't hear him. Such a clever speech!"

"I'm sure the *magid* spoke wonderfully," my father said. "But clever speech is no virtue, because the dull don't understand it, and the clever don't need it."

24

There were often disputes between us children. We were stubborn and refused to compromise. Once, our father said to us, "Brothers and sisters are like fingers of the same hand. No two fingers exactly alike, but if you bend them in a little, they all even out. Brothers and sisters must bend a bit too if they want to get along."

25

My father arranged lodgings in the city for the children in our family that were going to *kheyder*, or Jewish grade school. We would only come home during vacations or holidays.

My mother rarely traveled to the city, especially in the winter. She'd always tell us children to write. We promised to do so, but when it came to actually writing, we forgot completely. When she wanted to remind us, she'd ask my father to write us a letter. But these letters didn't help either.

Once, when my father came to the city, he went for a walk with me. On the street we ran into a Jew who said, "God be with you, Reb Hersh."

"And with you," my father answered.

A bit later my father asked me, "Did you hear what that man said?"

"Yes, he said, 'God be with you.'"

"And then what did I say?"

"You answered him, 'And with you.'"

"So it goes without saying, when someone speaks to you, you should respond?"

"Absolutely."

"A letter, my boy, is the same as speaking. Why, then, do you let your mother speak to you, and you don't answer?"

From that moment on, I never received a letter without responding right away.

26

Two Jews were arguing with each other in the tavern. One spoke quietly and the other shouted. My father tried to make peace between them and said to the one who was shouting, "What do you get out of this? You're a smart man after all."

"I can't stand stupidity!" the man yelled even louder.

"I understand," my father said. "But a smart man must be careful not to harm others with his intellect."

27

An old Jew, and a particularly depraved one, boasted that he still had the same virility he had in his youth. My father said to him, "An old man with a young man's drive is like a young colt hitched to an old wagon."

28

My father loved jokes, but he also knew when to be serious. Once, when he was having a more serious conversation, and someone interrupted with a joke, he said, "If one were to ask what it means to be a buffoon, wouldn't you say a buffoon is one who jokes when everyone else is trying to be serious?"

29

And another time he said, "There's no point in joking with someone you can't also be serious with."

30

If one of my brothers wanted to travel to the city to buy goods for the tavern, my father would sit with him the night before and make up a list. Once, in the morning before my brother's departure, my father mentioned something else he needed to buy. He told my brother to write it down.

"I don't need to write it down," my brother said. "I've got it in my head."

"And why would you want to fill your head with such petty things?" my father said. "Write it down."

31

A Jew came to ask a favor of my father. He spoke meekly. "Why do you insult me?" my father said.

"God forbid!" the man cried out. "How have I insulted you?"

"Absolutely you've insulted me. With such meekness one speaks only to a tyrant."

32

In our area there was a Jewish village merchant who had a nasty reputation. He was considered a dishonest man by all accounts. Because my father loathed gossip, he said that he refused to believe what anyone said about the man until the man himself convinced him otherwise. Eventually my father came to do business with the man. The man, aware of his reputation, immediately started defending himself to my father. My father said to the man, "Yes, I've certainly heard a lot of bad things about you. It could be that it's all just gossip. So I'll tell you what, I'll mark you down for one hundred. That is to say, I accept that you are one hundred percent honest. Now, if you should want to haggle me down from there, that's up to you."

33

One of my brothers, who studied at the university, was an ardent socialist. When he came home on break he'd speak constantly of socialism. Being a young student, and wanting to demonstrate his knowledge, he'd also speak about many other ideologies.

These matters weren't foreign to my father. But one time, when my brother got himself all riled up about these other ideologies, my father interjected with a parable.

"Once there was a golden coin. This coin, we call truth. People exchanged this coin for copper pennies. Now the world contains many ideals, but few truths."

34

Two wagon drivers who were taking grain to the city stopped by the tavern. My father noticed that one of them constantly used the phrase "in short." He quietly said to my mother, "I'm afraid of this fellow."

"What for?" my mother asked.

"Because a fellow that's always using the phrase 'in short' must bore people to death."

35

Someone was expressing regret over a falling out with a friend. My father said to him, "You don't always need to mourn over the loss of a friend; there are the kinds of friends that when you lose them it's really more of a gain."

36

"The patient wants to know how sick he is. The doctor wants to know how much health the patient has left."

37

"An honest person who tells a lie is like someone who walks crooked down a straight path. A liar who tells the truth is like someone who walks straight down a crooked path."

38

"When two weaklings meet, they become twice as weak as they were before."

39

"Don't search for true worth using false measures."

BIOGRAPHIES

Yitskhok (Isac) Horowitz (1893–1961) was a talented literary voice in American Yiddish culture. Editor, poet, playwright, translator, children's writer, vegetarian activist—Yitskhok Horowitz wore many hats in a life that led him from a village in Romania to New York and on to Los Angeles. *The Tavern of Popricani* represents one of the first translations of any of his works into English.

Ollie Elkus is a former 2020 Yiddish Book Center Translation Fellow. This volume is in part a result of his fellowship. *The Tavern of Popricani* is his first full-length published work. Most recently he has contributed to such notable projects as the Augustow Yizkor Book and the Ringelblum Archive's documents of the Warsaw Ghetto. He is a Yiddish translator of printed prose and poetry, as well as hand-written letters and postcards, but he also likes to play drums and drink tea. Ollie was born in Cincinnati in 1996 and currently lives in Detroit.

Ezra Finkin lives in Easton, Maryland, and is an illustrator of urban and nature scenes working in pen and ink and watercolor.